MW01598707

Because It Works!

Because It Works!

Writing How-To Articles from
New England Writers' Network.

To Peggy –
Write on!
Glenda Baker
June 2008

Glenda Baker

Copyright © 2008 by Glenda Baker.

Library of Congress Control Number: 2007906232
ISBN: Hardcover   978-1-4257-7799-9
               Softcover   978-1-4257-7795-1

All rights reserved. No part of this book may be reproduced or transmitted in any form
or by any means, electronic or mechanical, including photocopying, recording, or by any
information storage and retrieval system, without permission in writing from the copyright
owner.

This book was printed in the United States of America.

To order additional copies of this book, contact:
Xlibris Corporation
1-888-795-4274
www.Xlibris.com
Orders@Xlibris.com
39300

Contents

Sharing—Because Writers Need Other Writers

Other Genres—Because You Need to Stretch

The Next Step—Because It Doesn't Stop with the Writing

Finding Your Voice and Style—Because It's About You

Introduction

By Glenda Baker

From the first issue of *New England Writers' Network* (Summer 1994), we have included a **how-to** article on some aspect of writing in almost every issue. Because we editors are also writers and teachers of writing, our purpose has always been to see things from all sides of a three-sided desk. We have also worked very hard to be compassionate editors/critiquers, the kind *we* would like to work with when we submit our own writing.

If you have been an *NEWN* subscriber since the first issue, you have read all these articles. We hope that as a result you have applied our suggestions, improved your writing, and become a published writer. If you have, this book will be a review for you and a way to keep all our acquired wisdom at your fingertips. If you are new to *NEWN*, here are all the articles you missed. Read them. Follow our advice. Get published.

Our how-to's are not rules (although sometimes we can get emphatic). Our critiquing and teaching criteria have always been: does it work? If not, how can we make it work? So we offer these guidelines **because they work!**

At the end of each article we have added an assignment, most of which are based on taking a piece that doesn't work (we all have a drawer full of them) and applying what will make it work. We hope these assignments will produce many publishable stories and published writers—and clean out that drawer.

The articles are by Judy Adourian, poetry and personal essay; Liz Aleshire, fiction editor; and me, editor-in-chief and fiction editor.

We want to thank Berji Torres, Donna Bruno, Donna Ricci, Cathy Cairns, and Ann Hendricks for their help now and when the articles were originally published.

Because It Works! is dedicated to all our subscribers, contributors, submitters, students, and readers who have taught us more than we could have learned any other way.

Write on!

Glenda, Judy, and Liz

Visit *NEWN Magazine* at *www.newnmag.net*
Visit me at *www.glendabaker.com*
Visit Judy Adourian at *www.writeyes.com*
Visit Liz Aleshire at *www.lizaleshire.com*

"I've just read your article on point of view. WOW! Clear, concise, to the point, and in no way confusing . . . this is the best and easiest explanation I've seen."

—Arline Chase,
   author of Eppie finalists *Killraven* and *Ghost Dancer,*
   and of the Spirit Series, *Spirit of Earth* and *Spirit of Fire.*
   Instructor for Writer's Digest School.
   publisher@ebooksonthe.net

THE ELEMENTS OF FICTION WRITING—
BECAUSE THEY WORK

1

Who Are These People & What Are They Doing in My Story? Part 1

I was working on my novel one day when I suddenly heard a voice say, *"Bonjour!"*
"What?" I asked
"Bonjour," the voice repeated. *"Comment ça va?"*
"I'm sorry," I said, "but I don't speak French."
"Très bien. I speak English."
"Okay," I said, "but who are you and what are you doing in my story?"
"Oh, I'm Aunt Suzette from Paris."
"And you are in my story because . . ."
"In Chapter 3 you say Clarice she visit her Aunt Suzette in Paris when she is sixteen."
"Well, yeah, but that was just a passing comment . . ."
"I decide I *must* be in story."
"But you're not even a minor character. You were just a comment."
"I must tell my story! I was born in a little village outside of Paris . . ."
The next thing I knew I'd gotten off the track completely and was writing a whole different story than I had planned—and maybe that's the whole problem: I hadn't planned.

When I finally realized what was happening, I told Aunt Suzette emphatically that this was Clarice's story. She would have to pack up her bags and go back to Paris. But I also told her that I'd keep her on file in case I could use her in a future story. She wasn't very happy, but she did leave.

Have you ever had a character take over your story? I know it happens and now I know why it happens—because we haven't thought through who our characters are and why they do what they do. We haven't planned.

If you're writing a short story, you'll have to limit the number of characters. Short stories can run from fifty-five words to ten thousand words, but let's consider a story of about twenty-five hundred words. Two to three characters is a good guideline, although short stories have been written about one character and about considerably more than three.

Let's think about the main character, the one who wants something she can't have at the beginning of the story. She overcomes various obstacles so that by the end of the story she either has or hasn't obtained what she wants.

The main character (m.c.) answers the question "Whose story is this?" Usually the m.c. is also the point-of-view character, meaning we tell the story through the eyes, thoughts, and feelings of the m.c.

But the m.c. doesn't have to be the p.o.v. (point of view) character. The story may be told from the point of view of an observer who is watching and interpreting what he sees the m.c. do and say. For example, all of the Sherlock Holmes stories are told from Dr. Watson's p.o.v., making him the p.o.v. character while Holmes is the m.c.

The important thing in short stories is that we don't switch p.o.v. One p.o.v. per short story, please.

One of the main problems novice writers have is that even though they've thought up a character for a short story, the character doesn't want or need anything. No matter how interesting you think your m.c. is and no matter how many words you write, if your m.c. doesn't want something, there's no story. The essence of a short story is conflict and resolution—no conflict; no resolution; no story.

If you're writing a novel, you'll have lots of characters. They will be major, minor, or just passing through for a particular reason. How crucial they are to your story will determine how much you need to develop them. The important thing is that they should be well-rounded, meaning they must have weaknesses as well as strengths, vices as well as virtues. Gone are the days of the white hats (the good guys) versus the black hats (the bad guys). To be well-rounded, even the saint must have a weakness and his enemy must have some socially redeeming quality. The sweet little old lady has a greedy streak. The serial murderer rescues homeless kittens.

The easiest way to make sure your characters are well rounded is to make use of a tool called the character biography. Many books on fiction writing will give you a sample character bio form. This will include everything from physical description to hopes and fears, likes and dislikes, childhood memories, and what he eats for breakfast in the morning. Fill it in completely and you will have developed a well-rounded character, a character who you will know inside and out.

When I first saw Nancy Kress's character bio in *Dynamic Characters*, I thought it was much too long. Why did I have to know what my character's morning routine was? Why did I have to know what he ate for breakfast?

In the next scene I wrote, the m.c.'s wife had left him during the night. In the morning he got up and had to make his own breakfast. I *did* have to know what he ate for breakfast!

A character bio is a tool to use as needed. You may want to complete it before you start writing fiction. Or you may find that part way into the muddled middle you have lost track of what your m.c. wants or why she wants it. That's a great time to go back and review your character's bio or to complete it if you haven't already done so.

A character bio is also a good way to keep track of characters' names, physical descriptions, and all the little details that we must keep consistent.

Books and books and books have been written about developing fictional characters. Two of the best are *Dynamic Characters* by Nancy Kress and *Creating Characters* by Dwight Swain.

Because it works: Pick a story that isn't working for you and ask, "How well do I know my main character?" If you feel you don't know him or her (or any character) well enough, do a character bio. Also be sure to ask, "What does my main character want?" If you can't answer the question quickly or at all, this may be the reason the story isn't working. ❀

2

Who Are These People & What Are They Doing in My Story? Part 2

We've talked about who the characters in your story are. Now we have to talk about what they're doing there.

We do this through characterization: showing who the character is through his actions and reactions, his thoughts and feelings.

Here are some methods of characterization with examples:

1. **Direct explanation:** This is one way to let your reader know something about a character, but it isn't the best way because it's telling.
   Henry was an angry man.
2. **What the character thinks:** reporting direct thoughts that show Henry is angry.
   Junior slammed the door again, Henry thought. This time he's going to get it.
3. **What the character says:** reporting dialogue that shows anger through what Henry says and how he says it.
   "Do that one more time, Junior," Henry yelled, "and you'll wish you hadn't."
4. **Through the character's actions:** showing anger through what a character does.
   Henry slapped Junior.
5. **Through the character's motives and reactions:** showing anger through a character's reaction to something that happens.
   Junior let the back door slam waking Henry from a sound sleep. Henry jumped out of bed and ran downstairs to find his son.
6. **Through specific active details**: Show anger through description.
   The dent in the car fender was a result of Henry's rage at the driver of the blue Saturn who had cut him off on the way home from work. The hole in the living room wall was a result of Henry's last outburst at Junior.

7. **What another character tells us:** conversation between two other characters.

> *"Stay away from your father," Mom told Junior. "He had a bad day at work and he's in one of his moods."*
>
> *"What's with him, Mom? I never can do anything right."*
>
> *"He's just tired. His job is stressful right now."*
>
> *"It's always stressful!" Junior slammed his algebra book on the kitchen table. "He's hated me since the day I was born."*
>
> *Mom went to the sink, turned the water on, and began washing the supper dishes, clanking the dishes together. "Damn!" Mom said as she removed two halves of a plate from the sudsy water.*

8. **Through a word, a look, a move, or a gesture:** mannerisms and patterns of mannerisms.

> *The vein on Henry's temple always throbbed visibly when he was about to blow.*
>
> Or, *When Dad tapped his fingers on the table, Junior knew he was in for trouble.*

These examples show the reader that Henry is an angry man without telling. Any, or a combination of all of these examples, could be used in a story.

Even as I wrote these examples, I could see the beginning of a story. I want to know why Henry is so angry. I also want to know why Mom won't talk to Junior about his father (or is he really Junior's father—if not, why did they name him Junior?). She's obviously trying to protect Junior by warning him of his father's mood, but what's her secret and why did she break a plate? Is she angry too—or scared?

Let's try another one:

1. **Direct explanation:**

> *Eunice was in love.*

2. **What the character thinks:**

> *I've never felt like this before, Eunice thought. Sebastian is the most romantic man I've ever met.*

3. **What the character says:**

> *"I just can't stop thinking about him, Sylvia. I can't sleep or eat or concentrate at work."*

4. **Through the character's actions:**

> *Eunice bought the black lace teddy on display in the window of Victoria's Secret.*

5. **Through the character's motives and reactions:**

> *Eunice let the phone ring three times before she answered it. Her heart pounded; her hand trembled as she picked up the receiver.*
>
> *"Hello," she said, trying to control the quaver in her voice.*
>
> *"Are you happy with your long-distance carrier?" a voice asked.*

6. **Through specific active details:**

> *When she'd moved into the apartment, Eunice had painted her bedroom pink—the pink of party dresses, strawberry ice cream, and cotton candy. The color she would choose for her bridesmaids' dresses and the tea roses in her bridal bouquet.*

7. **What another character tells us:**

> *"Eunice is crazy about him," Sylvia said. "She really thinks he's going to marry her."*
>
> *"She doesn't know he **is** married?" Pam slowly stirred her tea.*
>
> *"She thinks he's divorced—or about to be."*
>
> *"Who's going to tell her?"*
>
> *"Don't look at me!" Sylvia tossed her napkin onto the table. "That girl's in love with love, and I'm not going to be the one to shatter her illusion."*

8. **Through a word, a look, a move, or a gesture:**

> *"Oh, I'm very happy with my long-distance server," Eunice said as calmly as she could, then hung up the phone. Sebastian wasn't going to call. She went to the bar and poured herself a glass of sherry, the same thing she always did when she finally admitted he would never call.*

So there you go, another exercise that started out as a series of examples and ended up being at least the beginnings of a story.

Because it works: Now it's your turn. Give it a try. Pick a character and an emotion, then take that character through the eight characterization examples and see what you come up with. Your writing will definitely be more exciting. ❊

3

In the Beginning . . .

"Once upon time . . ."

"In a galaxy far, far away . . ."

"It was a dark and stormy night . . ."

How *do* you start a story?

Before we can decide how to start the story, we have to decide *where* to start.

"Just start at the very beginning," you say. "That's a very good place to start."

"Maybe," I say, "and maybe not."

Let's experiment with several openings to a story to see what works and what doesn't. Our story will be about a city girl's first visit to the farm where her boyfriend grew up. Do we start by telling the reader how Sam and Vanessa met? When they're on the way to the farm? When Sam introduces Vanessa to his mom? Or how Vanessa was scared by a rooster when she was five years old? Let's try a possible opening and see what happens:

Vanessa had been dating Sam for six months. She had met him at a seminar in New York City. The first time Sam saw Vanessa he thought she was beautiful, just the kind of girl he'd been looking for. After the seminar they went out for coffee. Vanessa hoped Sam would call her. He did. They dated for six months and then he asked her if she'd like to meet his mom on the farm in Iowa he grew up on. Vanessa said okay even though she didn't really like farms. Suddenly a rooster crowed and woke her up.

Problem: This is a summary opening. Many writers feel they must tell the whole background story in the first paragraph, which usually ends up being several paragraphs, if not pages. Not a good idea. Usually background can be woven in later; sometimes much of the back-story isn't needed at all.

When the story opens, we don't need to know how Vanessa and Sam met. What we do need to know is: where does this story take place, who's there, a basic understanding of what's happening, and at least a hint of conflict. In this opening, we might assume the characters are in the city where they met. If so, how did the rooster get there?

Although there is a hint of conflict (Vanessa doesn't like farms), it's not clear who the p.o.v. character is because we have thoughts from both Sam and Vanessa. Or maybe the rooster is telling the story.

So let's try again.

"Are we there yet?" she asked as they passed another barren winter field. Dried corn stalks lay broken by the cold wind. In the distance the gunmetal gray sky threatened snow. Even inside his warm car, she shivered.

Problem: There's some description of a cornfield in winter, which may or may not be essential to the story, but the main problem is The Pronoun Problem—pronouns with no antecedents to refer to. Who are *they*? Who is *she*? Whose car is she in?

Another try:

"Time to get up," Sam said.

"What do you mean?" Vanessa asked. "It's the middle of the night." Vanessa buried her head in her pillow. A rooster had just crowed to announce the dawn and had wakened them.

Problem: We don't know a whole lot more with this opening. But the main problem is the order of the information. Every scene needs an action followed by a reaction. In this opening the action (the rooster crowing) comes after the response (waking up).

Let's try again:

Vanessa decided to tell him as soon as he came in from the barn.

"I can't stand it here another minute," she said.

"What?" Sam Burns said.

"I said I can't stand it here. I wasn't cut out for farm life."

Damn, Sam thought, I was afraid of this. "Well," he said, "it's only for two more days." He didn't want her to know how disappointed he was.

Problem: This opening gives us a little more information. We know who the characters are, where they are, and there's definitely a hint of conflict, but it's confusing because it's not clear who the p.o.v. character is. Again we have thoughts from both Vanessa and Sam.

In the opening of a story, we must present the facts, the *status quo*, as quickly and as concisely as possible. We begin the story where the *status quo* is just about to change. A letter arrives. The phone rings. A body is found. A rooster crows.

"Cock-a-doodle-do!"

The rooster's strident crow woke Vanessa up with a start.

"What the . . . ?" she said.

"Rooster," Sam mumbled.

"But it's the middle of the night!" Vanessa buried her head in her pillow.

"Sun's coming up." Sam was out of bed before the words were out of his mouth. "Time to help with the milking," he added with enthusiasm.

"What?"

"Come on, honey," Sam urged, "you can help Mom make breakfast."

"Breakfast?" Vanessa groaned. "I haven't eaten breakfast since I was in grammar school." What have I gotten myself into? she wondered.

This opening grounds the reader. We know:

1.   Story contains at least three characters: Sam, Vanessa, and Mom.
2.   Time: Early morning.
3.   Place: on a farm.
4.   Action: Two people waking up in the morning.
5.   P.O.V. character: Vanessa.
6.   They are at Sam's Mom's house where he is very comfortable with the routine.
7.   Conflict: Vanessa isn't happy about being woken at dawn or about being at the farm.

That's a lot of information to put into a few opening sentences, but with a little practice and experimentation, it can be done.

There are many ways to begin a story. We can start with:

Dialogue:

"Tom!"

No answer.

"Tom!"

No answer.

"What's gone with that boy, I wonder? You Tom!"—From *The Adventures of Tom Sawyer* by Mark Twain.

Action:

Someone must have been telling lies about Joseph, for without having done anything wrong he was arrested one fine morning.—From *The Trial* by Franz Kafka.

Description of a place or an item that is pertinent to the story:

The Salinas Valley is in Northern California. It is a long, narrow swale between two ranges of mountains and the Salinas River winds and twists up the center until it falls at last into Monterey Bay.—From *East of Eden* by John Steinbeck.

Statement of theme:

It was the best of times, it was the worst of times, it was the age of wisdom, and it was the age of foolishness . . .—from *A Tale of Two Cities* by Charles Dickens.

Even though these are examples of the openings of novels, they are excellent classic beginnings.

There are lots of ways to start a story, but there are two no-nos.

(1) Do not start with "It was . . ." (Yes, I know Dickens did.)
(2) Do not start with a weather report. Here is an example containing both:

It was a hot morning in late August. The sun was just starting to rise over the ocean like a big red ball. The water was calm and smooth. The sand was still hot because the night air hadn't cooled it off at all. A lone seagull was walking on the sand. Suddenly it squawked, flapped its wings and flew away. Mabel enjoyed the morning solitude. It looked like a scene from a postcard, but this morning something just didn't feel right.

Because this opening is all telling, it's boring and sounds simplistic. After reading only that much, most editors would immediately reject the manuscript. We need to pull the reader into the story by **showing** what's happening. Weave the weather into the action.

"Eighty degrees already," Mabel mumbled as she watched the crimson sun rise slowly over the ocean. "Must be the hottest August on record." She walked quickly over the sand, still hot from yesterday's scorching sun, to the water's edge and let the gentle wavelets cool her bare toes. A lone seagull strutting along the shore squawked as she approached, then flapped his wings and flew off.

Mabel took a long, deep breath of the salty air and exhaled slowly. Her morning walk on the shore usually relaxed her, prepared her for the day, but this morning something just didn't feel right. The sun now glowed full and red above the horizon.

"Red sky in the morning," Mabel said, "sailors take warning."

There's one more question we need to discuss about beginnings. How long is a beginning?

Answer: That depends on how long the story is. The shorter the story, the tighter the opening must be. If the editor isn't drawn into the story by the end of the first page (which is actually more like a half a page), she won't turn the page to read further.

In *The Guide to Editing Your Fiction* Michael Seidman says to draw the reader into the story by ". . . giving her something to care about, something to intrigue or entice, something to pull her in and make her wonder." Compel her to turn the page.

Every so often an opening line will come to you in a flash and you'll know it's perfect. Other times you'll rewrite the opening a hundred times before you're satisfied with it. But as we all know: Writing is rewriting.

Starting with something as simple as "Once upon time . . ." is a way to warm up, get the juices flowing. But be sure to delete it from your final draft.

Because it works: Experiment by writing at least three different openings for your next story. Five is even better. Try some of these ways to begin:

1. Jump right into the action. Something happens to the main character and s/he reacts.
2. A brief description of some object that will be important in the story.
3. Several lines of dialogue between two characters who are arguing about something that will happen in the story.
4. A description of the setting where the first scene occurs. Concentrate on what is significant about the setting or how the setting influences the main

character. [If you start with a weather report, there'd better be a hurricane coming!]

5. An outrageous opinion held by the main character—expressed in her head in her own words. Something she would never tell a living soul.

Don't worry about whether you like any of your beginnings or not, or even if any one of them actually ends up being your beginning.

These ideas are based on information from *Beginnings, Middles, and Endings* by Nancy Kress. ❀

4

What's Happening? Part 1

Rose, a student in my fiction-writing class, is reading the opening scene of her novel to the class. She finishes the two-thousand-word piece, and everybody murmurs and nods their heads.

I wait for the rest of the class to look up from their copies and make comments.

"I like your description," somebody finally says.

"Yeah," someone else adds, "I felt like I was right there."

"I think on page 3 you want *its*, not *it's*," someone else offers.

"I liked that her cat's name was Putter Puss," another adds.

I let the class make comments like these for a few more minutes, and I say, "Okay, these are all valid comments, but what's missing?"

I let the silence hang in the room for thirty seconds that seem like several minutes, then ask, "What has happened in the two thousand words that Rose has written?"

More silence,

Cautiously, a brave soul says, "Well, the description of the red purse was great and we know that the main character is an orphan and that she has a calico cat and that she drives a 1998 red Mustang and that the Halloween she was five she was so scared by her brother's Dracula costume that she wet her pants."

"Is this enough to hook the reader, the first one of whom will be the editor of a publication that Rose hopes will publish the story?" I ask.

Silence.

Finally, I say, "Let's boil down what's actually happened in this opening scene: The main character woke up, had breakfast, fed her cat, found her keys, and drove to work."

Everybody nods.

"But what's happened?" I ask again. "Nothing." I answer my own question gently.

"But she has to get to work because she's going to ask for a raise today," Rose says.

"Then why not start the story with the main character (affectionately known as m.c.) at work nervously waiting outside the boss's office, getting up the courage to go in? Do we really need to know what she had for breakfast, that she has a red purse, or what happened when she was five?"

"I guess not," Rose answers, then asks, "Then do I flashback to tell how poor she was as a kid and how she decided she'd never be poor again?"

"What if instead of a flashback, she goes into his office?" I suggest.

"Oh."

I continue. "Then maybe as she's trying to ask for a raise, her boss is continually interrupted by phone calls and other people, and she is getting more and more nervous and annoyed."

"Then she gets the raise," Rose says.

"Well, if she gets the raise, all is well and where does the story go from there?"

No comments.

"In any scene," I say, "but especially the opening scene, the reader needs to have something to wonder about, to care about. There has to be even a hint of conflict."

"Oh, that comes later," Rose insists, "when she has to decide whether or not to give up her career as a hula hoop instructor to marry the billionaire from New Zealand. Should I put that in the first scene?"

"Probably not. Now you're starting at the end of the story. Let's talk about where to start a story and how to hook the reader in the opening paragraphs."

I experience this same scenario often when working with novice writers. I call it The Nothing's Happening Syndrome.

So what do we do about it?

1. Every scene must have a purpose.
2. Every scene must advance the story.
3. Every scene must give the reader something to be concerned about, must have some tension, some suspense, i.e. must have conflict even if it isn't the main conflict of the entire short story or novel.

Let's look at my student's example: a woman about to ask for a raise. In a short story, we might start with the m.c. outside her boss's office practicing what she's going to say, making sure she looks perfect, worrying because the boss is late, whatever *shows* her anxiety.

She finally gets in to see her boss, but he is continually interrupted. All the while the reader's concern is if she'll get her raise. By the end of a short story she will overcome the obstacles and quite probably will get the raise. The reader will sigh with relief and be satisfied.

If, in our short story, m. c. doesn't get the raise, something else good quite probably will happen. The boss will tell her he's always loved her and Putter Puss and that he wants to marry her and support them both "forever." Or in a more literary story she may decide that the good works she's doing saving orphan cats is more important than money so she doesn't need the raise and can live on warm, fuzzy feelings.

If we use this same scene in a novel, however, one of three things can happen:

1. **"No**, you can't have the raise." If the story is going to continue, she now has to come up with some other way to get the money she needs.
2. **"No**, you can't have the raise, **and besides** that you're fired." Now, not only does she not get the raise, she has no job. The stakes are raised because she's in a worse predicament than when she started.
3. **"Yes,** I'll give you the raise, **but** you have to work weekends." (Or "I'm moving you to the office in East Overshoe." Or "You have to sleep with me." Or something equally as dastardly.) Now the m.c. has a real dilemma: she can have what she wants, but is she willing to pay the price?

Hooking the reader with a fantastic opening line is essential to a piece of fiction, but don't stop there. Make something happen immediately! Readers want to know what situation the m.c. is in and what she wants (even if only in this scene) before they care about her childhood, her red purse, or her cat's name.

Because it works: Analyze each scene from a story that isn't working and determine if it ends with a **Yes**. Determine how you can raise the stakes to make a **No**, a **No, besides** or a **Yes, but** ending. Sometimes it's just a matter of making the scene a little longer or stopping it a little earlier. ❋

5

What's Happening? Part 2

Now let's look at a synopsis of a fictional short story that we'll call "Unfinished Business." The actual story, we'll say, is 3,500 words and is written in the first person, past tense. We can break this story down into seven scenes that we'll look at individually to determine what's happening in each scene.

Scene 1: Frank returns home to Massachusetts after getting out of the Army and before he's going to start a job at XYZ Corp. in California. He has everything he owns in his car.

His mother is painting the fence and is very surprised that Frank has returned earlier than she expected. During the conversation, Frank swears several times which offends his mother. Frank unloads his car, chats with his mother, and smokes a cigarette, which also offends her. Mother is not happy that Frank will be moving across the country.

Scene 2: Frank then goes to his father's hardware store where he worked as a teenager. His father happily greets him. Business is slow, so Dad closes the shop early and he and Frank go home to have supper.

Scene 3: After supper Frank and Mother catch up on what's happened around town since Frank joined the Army. His parents want to know more about his new job and where he'll be living, but Frank doesn't have any details.

Scene 4: Frank decides to take a walk and follows the route he used to walk to high school. He reflects on his school days.

Scene 5: Frank continues on to the soccer field behind the school where two teams of the town's soccer league are playing. He watches the game and remembers several players from high school. He also notices several girls watching the game—one is Mona Schmidt, a former girlfriend.

When the game is over, Frank approaches Mona, who is happy to see him. They chat about high school, and Mona invites him to go to the bar where they all congregate after the soccer games. He decides to go.

Scene 6: They go to the bar. Mona introduces Frank to some of her friends, they have a couple of beers, and Mona chats with her friends until Frank gets bored and suggests they leave. They leave and drive out to the lake.

Scene 7: They have sex, then Mona says she has to go because her husband will miss her. Frank says his folks will be wondering where he is, too. Mona takes Frank home, drops him off in the driveway, and leaves. Frank wonders what will happen when he gets to California. The End.

What happened in 3,500 words? **Nothing!**

In this story, as described in this synopsis, there is absolutely no conflict, therefore, nothing to be resolved. "Unfinished Business" is a series of episodes with no thread tying them all together. We are left wondering what happened. The answer again is—**nothing**.

From the title we immediately want to know what the "Unfinished Business" is. There are so many possibilities, but there is no follow-through for any of them. Here are some questions we're left with:

Is there a problem between Frank and his parents?

Is Frank torn between taking the job with XYZ Corp. and possibly staying at home to help his father run the hardware store?

Is there some issue with his mother?

Is Mona a girl who jilted Frank in high school?

Is Mona's husband a classmate who stole Mona away from Frank? The fact the Mona is married might be something to include earlier in the story, maybe when they meet at the soccer game.

Who is Frank? What does he want? Why can't he have it?

Why should we even care about Frank?

Every scene in a work of fiction (no matter its length) must have some conflict—some tension which logically leads to the next scene, i.e. cause and effect. Something must happen in scene A (cause) that leads to the main character taking some action (effect) that leads to something else happening (scene B).

Let's say that the unfinished business is that just before high school graduation after which Frank entered the Army, Mona broke up with him without telling him why. During his four years in the Army, Frank wondered what happened. His letters went unanswered; he received no word from Mona.

When he arrives home, he asks Mom if she knows anything about Mona. Mom evades the question. There may be additional tension around the issue of Frank's job on the other side of the country. As Frank walks by the school, all kinds of memories of Mona can arise. When he finally sees her at the soccer game, the tension rises to a peak. He confronts her and she finally tells him why she broke up with him. The conflict is resolved and Frank gets what he wanted (an answer, happy or unhappy), the business is finished, and the reader is satisfied.

There are many other ways this story could develop, as many ways as people who might write it. Maybe the conflict is between Frank and his father whose hardware store is failing so he wants Frank to join him and use his MBA knowledge to revive the business. Frank, of course, wants to take the new job on the West Coast. The conflict could also be between Frank and Mona's husband, Billy Joe, who was Frank's best friend until Frank went into the Army and Billy Joe stole Mona. Frank needs to resolve what happened with Billy Joe.

The point is that something has to happen or you don't have a story.

If you're having trouble deciding what's happening in your story, here's a tool to use to determine what is (or isn't) happening. (See chart.) Read each scene and then put an X in the zone that applies.

Major dramatic action in Zone 1 would be murder, mayhem, or major happiness. "He loves me!" or "You just won the lottery!" In a short story there should be only one major dramatic action, and it will probably start the story.

Zone 2 are scenes of continuing forward action or flashbacks (dramatized scenes of previous action). The major part of a novel will contain mostly Zone 2 scenes that are comprised of obstacles and challenges to be overcome by the main character so he can (or does not) obtain what he wants.

Zone 3 scenes are for characterization, description, or backfill (backfill being previous information the reader needs but is narrated not dramatized).

Zone 4 is the BAD zone! These scenes contain words, words, words, but nothing happens. You should have NO X's in Zone 4. If you do, these scenes need to be rewritten so that they fall into any of the other zones.

Granted, some scenes will contain a combination of action, characterization, description, and backfill. The "Is Anything Happening?" chart is a tool to keep you on the track and to keep your story moving forward with action.

Whether you are writing a novel, novella, or short story, take the time to analyze each scene to determine what happens. If nothing does, you need to make something happen or to delete that scene and find another way to include any pertinent information.

For a complete study of the structure, type, and content of scenes, I highly recommend *The Novelist's Essential Guide to Crafting Scenes* by Raymond Obstfeld published by Writer's Digest Books.

What's Happening?

Zone 1:
  Major Dramatic
    Action

Zone 2:
  Dramatic Forward
  Action or Flashback

Zone 3:
  Characterization
  Or Backfill

Zone 4: Words but no
  Action or
  Characterization

DEAD   ZONE

1   2   3   4   5   6   7   8
                Scene

Because it works: Using the chart above, plot where each scene in one of your stories fits. Do you have more than *one major action* scene? Do you have any scenes in the Zone 4—THE DEAD ZONE? If you do, now is the time to rewrite them so they fall into Zones 2 or 3. ✻

6

Plodding Through the Plotting

Let's take a trip. Let's drive from Massachusetts to California, more specifically from Hudson, Massachusetts to Los Angeles, California. We'll have to do a lot of planning: When will we go? How long will it take? Should we take the clunker with 90,000 miles on it or rent a car? How far is it to LA, anyhow? Who's going to drive when? Will we stop along the way or drive right through? Where will we spend the night if we do stop? Should we drop in on Aunt Bessie in Iowa? Does Aunt Bessie still live in Iowa? When was the last time we heard from Aunt Bessie? I think it was 198 . . . Oops, I'm off on a tangent already. Do we even go through Iowa? What should we take with us? Or would it be better just to fly? And on and on and on.

Or maybe we should get in the car, head west, and see where we are when we hit the Pacific Ocean. We might be in LA or San Diego or San Francisco. What difference does it make? We'll be in California and maybe something exciting will happen wherever we end up.

How does this trip relate to writing? I'm sure you figured that out long before we got to Iowa. Plotting is a plan. That's all: How am I going to get from the beginning of the story I want to tell to the end?

I could have started this article with, "There are two kinds of writers . . ." Well, there are. In this case there are those who plot out their entire piece of writing, and then there are those who start a piece and have no plan as to where it's going until they get to the end. And of course, there's everybody in the middle, all those writers who do some degree of plotting at some point in their writing process.

The plotters are those who plan every step of their story. They need to know exactly how and when everything's going to happen before they write a word.

The plodders, on the other hand, get an idea, start writing, and may be surprised where they end up.

So let's take a look at how we might plot a story. Here are the possible events in the life a fictional character.

1. A child is born. (Preemie? Late? Small? Huge?)
2. Childhood: Character learns to contend with siblings or with being an only child. (How many older/younger? Genders)
3. Child gets lost in supermarket at age 3. (With which parent? How does parent respond? How does this influence child? At the time? Later in life?)
4. Enters kindergarten early. (Why? What influence do parents have on this decision?)
5. Character tries out for sports, joins Scouts or some other social group. (Successful? Failure? Influence at time? Later in life?)
6. As teenager, character has first date. (Success or embarrassment?)
7. Gets driver's license. (Positive or negative result?)
8. Has problems with peers. (Bullied or bully?)
9. Grades change. (Up or down?)
10. Gets part in school play. (Success or embarrassment?)
11. Dates same person for all of high school. (How do parents feel about this person?)
12. Applies to college. (Gets into first choice college? Isn't accepted anywhere?)
13. Graduates from high school. (Class standing?)
14. Goes to college and majors in accounting as suggested by parent(s). (Where?)
15. Meets future spouse. (Who? When? Where? Details.)
16. Gets married. (Conditions?)
17. Has family. (How many kids?)
18. Suffers from a medical condition. (Depression? AIDS? Allergies?)
19. Works for twenty years at same job. (What job? Happy or dissatisfied?)
20. Returns to school to get Master's degree. (Satisfying?) (Frustrating?)
21. Loses spouse. (Death? Divorce?)
22. Becomes depressed. (Seriously? Contemplates suicide?)
23. Attends high school reunion. (New lease on life? Becomes more depressed?)

These twenty-two events are major life points. They are the chronological story of the main character's life and are emotionally neutral. If you were to write the life story of the m.c., would you write it chronologically? Probably not. If you were to write a novel (a fictionalized story) based on the m.c.'s life, would you write it chronologically, i.e. starting with the m.c.'s birth and recounting every event in her life in order? I probably wouldn't start with m.c.'s birth unless it was unique or eventful in some way. Read *Wicked* by Gregory Maguire or *David Copperfield by* Charles Dickens, or *Catcher in the Rye* by J. D. Salinger.

The suggestions in parentheses give you choices to make about those life events (plot points), options to add conflict and, hence, make a story rather than just a chronology. So how *would* I write the story of M.C.'s life?

Whether I wrote the story as fiction or nonfiction, I would rearrange the events to make M.C.'s life more exciting, more dramatic, more readable. I could start the story at whatever point I wanted depending on what I wanted to emphasize. I might start when M.C. was in the middle of her depression and make it a story of how she dug herself out. How did she do it? How long did it take? I could start the story when M.C. decided to go back to school. Why did she decide to return to school? What's it like to be an adult student? What obstacles did she have to overcome? Did the fact that she started kindergarten early influence her decision to return to college as an adult?

I might decide to start the story when M.C. meets her former boyfriend at the reunion and flashback to their love story in high school. Why did they break up? What does she think about him now?

There's also a theme running through these plot points. Did you catch it? Several places I wrote that choices were made because of the wishes of a parent. What influence did that parent have on M.C.'s life? Did she rebel over her parent's wishes? Or did she always do what she was told to do?

Wherever you decide to start M.C.'s story, you should begin where the status quo is about to change. If M.C.'s depression is the story you want to write, you might start with the event that starts her depression or at the point where she is just about to kill herself. But wherever you start, make sure you start when something major is about to happen. You want the reader to keep turning the pages to find out whether or not M.C. gets what she wants.

Obviously, the longer the story, the more plotting you have to do. Short fiction writers may be able to think through their story idea without writing out the plan, while those who write longer fiction may need to write long, detailed plot plans.

You may also plot the story whenever you wish. Elizabeth George plots her English mysteries in much detail before she begins to write. Raymond Obstfeld (author of many novels and how-to books) plots the first third of his novels, writes it, plots the second third, writes that, then plots and writes the last third.

The more complex the story, the more plotting you need to do. (I wonder how long it took Dan Brown to plot out *The Da Vinci Code*.) Mystery writers have to know "who dunnit" so they can plant all the clues and red herrings along the way. Yes, I know sometimes things change during the writing; but without some kind of a plan you could get as lost in your story as you could if you headed to California without a map.

"But if I plan everything out," I hear you say, "I'll lose spontaneity and excitement." And my answer is, *not necessarily*. If you're excited about your idea, plotting your story means planning it for the *most* exciting presentation. There will also be places where you're not exactly sure how something will happen. M.C. needs to find out information about whether her mother suffered from depression, but you don't know how she'll obtain that information. That plot point would read, "Somehow M.C. finds the info. she needs." It's those "somehows" that keep your creativity flowing.

Writers who say they don't plot probably do a lot of planning in their heads even if they don't write a formal plot list.

In the most general sense, a plot is just a "list of what you *think* is going to happen in the order you *think* they are going to happen." Liz Aleshire calls it *sequencing*. But whatever you call it, don't get hung up on a formal outline. Put events in the order you think you're going to use them and then start writing. Nothing is carved in stone. Everything is subject to change—even "who dunnit."

So give yourself a map to California so you'll stay on track and not end up in Canada.

Because it works: Before you start writing your next story, make a list of the events that you think are going to happen in the order you think they are going to happen. Use it as a guideline when you write the story. Did the list help you stay on track? If you wandered off, did going back to the list help you get back on track? ❋

7

What's the Story Question?

A reader who isn't satisfied with the answer to a story's question is disappointed. A writer who can't find a unique way to answer an age-old story question is frustrated.

So what is a story question? It's an essential, though unrecognized, part of writing any story, book, article, or essay. It's unrecognized because it's so obvious we, as writers, constantly overlook it. The story question is the plot line's inherent demand to know HOW? The story question is the writer's demand to know WHY? The story question is the reader's demand to know both.

No, the story question is not theme. Theme should be distilled down to one or two words: greed, lust, unrequited love, hope, courage. This isn't an article about theme, but I must point out here that theme is as much a function of the writer's intent as it is the reader's experience. A writer may write a story with the intentional theme of unrequited love. A reader may experience the story as being about hope. Or loss. Or consequences. Both are right. It is the mark, in my opinion, of the truly proficient and creative writer to produce a story with a theme that is recognized by the reader exactly as the writer intended. But that isn't required. Writing should make us think. If that means, as readers, our experience shows us a different theme than the writer intended, or a slightly different perspective of that theme, then the author has also done her work.

Theme is another often overlooked aspect of story telling. We don't always sit down at the typewriter or PC to write about greed, lust, love, hope, or courage. We are compelled to write a story. When we get proficient enough at our art to manipulate a story to convey theme, then we can pat ourselves on the back for a job superbly well done. I don't believe there is, or has been, any writer who always begins a story from a theme.

So, if the story question isn't theme, what is it? Let's start with the plot story question. Actually, let's start with a discussion of plot. You do know, don't you, that there are no new stories in the world? Well, it's true. Human nature hasn't changed much over the centuries, so our basic human experiences haven't changed either. Instinct still drives us all; and as long as it does, our stories will have the same basic plot lines. There are only four stories to tell: man against man, man against nature, man against himself, and man against society, The most basic of these and most often used, is:

> Boy meets girl.
> Boy loses girl.
> Boy gets girl.

How then do we create from the same, constant plot lines stories that are both unique and bring a new perspective to the reader? By answering the inherent plot question of HOW?

The fact that boy meets girl is constant, but how he meets the girl is dependent on our own experience and creativity. Since we are unique, basic human instincts notwithstanding, we can bring a unique perspective to these old plot lines. Subconsciously, writers have been doing this since we first told stories by drawing pictures depicting the hunt on cave walls. Surely all prehistoric food hunts were the same: they went, they found, they killed. But we know from current day research that each observer on that hunt could have seen the day's events in very different ways. Just delve into several eyewitness accounts of the same crime and you'll find this is true.

Answering the HOW part of the story question as it relates to plot is the first step a writer takes in creating a story. All too often this step is as unconscious, instinctual, and overlooked as theme. Many times, a story comes to us "full blown." We thank the gods for providing it that way because we remember the last forty-seven stories we slogged through just to get started—much less finish. Sometimes the HOW question is answered only after we've gotten sufficiently "into" a story to recognize the way it should go to match our intentions for writing it. I'd like to advocate that we pay more attention to the HOW question of plot line. If we were to play with a story with the awareness that we're looking for an answer to how the story should unfold, I believe we'd have more successes with our writing. We'd more often achieve that "aah" kind of satisfaction we got into writing to find in the first place.

Some writers (the ones we seem to hear from the most in magazines and on talk shows) will tell you that intentional writing takes the spark and life out of a story. I propose that unintentional writing means the reader has to wade through long, diverting, and boring beginnings that, in essence, tell us the story before the writer gets around to showing us the story. It's my rule of thumb, stolen from some other educator whose name I've since forgotten, that the first three pages of a short story can probably be cut without hurting it. Carla Neggers (author of dozens of romances and several mainstream novels) calls these slow beginnings authorial throat clearing. I agree. Simply because we, the writers, need to know a character's history and roots, doesn't mean the reader needs to know every one of those details up front. If truth be known, writing is probably more a process of knowing what to cut than it is what to put in. Write these beginnings to use as a tool to get to answer the HOW of the story question and then cut them from your final version.

So far we've established that the inherent plot question is HOW? How will the boy meet the girl? How will the boy lose the girl? How will the boy get the girl? Answering the HOW plot question uniquely will satisfy the need of the reader to have a story with a beginning, middle, and an end. Whether those are logical, illogical, rational, or irrational isn't relevant. A beginning, middle, and satisfying ending are only tools we use to convey our theme. Once this is done, we can get on to the fun stuff.

The fun stuff, the really fun question of writing a story, is discovering the WHY? Answering the HOW is strictly a convenience for the reader and a tool for the writer.

Answering the WHY question is the writer's sole domain. Though human, we are all unique. No one else on earth has lived exactly our life, hence, no one else on earth can tell our story the way we can! To make a story uniquely our own, we need to ask ourselves WHY we're telling this particular story in this particular way. Can you write a story without knowing WHY you're writing it? Of course. Will that story be inexplicably better when you know WHY you're writing it? Of course, again. I suggest we writers always take a little time to find out why we're writing a story. Is it to express our own perception of courage? Of greed? Of love? Of hope? Of loss? Where did the story come from? An experience from our past? Did this experience spur us on to write a story that has little or no comparison to the actual events yet expresses the emotions of those events? Whoops! Are we back to theme? Sure we are!

How do we find out WHY we're writing a story? Simple. Just answer this question: I'm writing this story because I feel _____ (I remember; I saw; I experienced; I want to) by filling in the blank at the end. And remember, "because I want to" or "because I have to" are valid answers. Just remember to go back when your story is done and try to unravel WHY you wrote it. Answering the WHY of our story question teaches us how to be intentional about our writing by making us conscious of the personal experience we're writing about. If you can't readily answer the WHY question, write a first draft and explore the story by looking back on it.

So why is WHY so important? Only by knowing WHY can we develop and complete a story that is satisfying to both the reader and the writer. If the writer knows WHY he's writing a story, he can hone it, prune it, symbolize it, metaphor it, describe it, enrich it—manipulate it—intentionally so that the end result conveys a theme instantly recognizable to any reader. Knowing WHY, combined with practice and writing experience, means the reader can get only the theme the writer intended. Whether or not we always achieve this isn't as important as striving to do so. If we write about love but the reader perceives greed, this is yet another bit of information we can learn from to further our process of becoming the best writers we can be.

Let's look at a specific example: We all know the story of Ebenezer Scrooge in Dickens' *A Christmas Carol*. We would probably all agree that the theme of the story is greed and miserliness. So the plot question, the HOW, is: How does Scrooge become aware of his miserliness? How do I, the writer, show Scrooge becoming aware of his problem and wanting to change? Answer: through a series of ghosts who **show** (not tell) Scrooge how he's ruined his life. The story question, the WHY, is then: Why would Scrooge want to change? What is his motivation to change? Answer: when he realizes that nobody will even miss him after he dies.

A writer's job is to communicate individual perspective in the hopes that the reader is spurred on to think about it. Answering the HOW question of the story's plot is by far the easier of the two. I stress that the HOW question must always be answered to make a story satisfying to the reader—and to convince an editor to print it. The WHY question is harder and may take years of work to achieve. But the WHY question makes the HOW infinitely more satisfying and complete.

So, the three basic rules of story writing, *à la* Liz, are:

> Never disappoint the reader with a weak answer to the HOW plot question.
> Never frustrate yourself by not knowing WHY you're writing your story.
> And always strive to enjoy the process.

Because it works: Find one of your stories that isn't working. Using Liz's three basic rules, determine which rule you need to concentrate on. ✳

Article by Liz Aleshire

8

What Do I Show? What Do I Tell?

"*S*how; Don't Tell!"
"Show; Don't Tell!"
"Show; Don't Tell!"

We've all heard it until we want to scream. Entire books have been written on this topic alone. Do we really need another article on show; don't tell?

Absolutely.

Granted, every story is told *and* shown. To completely understand how to do this most effectively, let's start with the basics and look at the four kinds of writing:

1. Exposition: an explanation of facts, events, or ideas.
2. Description: writing involving the senses and feelings.
3. Narration: a connected succession of events.
4. Argument: persuasion to convince the reader of the "rightness" of certain ideas and the "wrongness" of others.

The purpose of creative writing (fiction, personal essays, and poetry) is not to explain facts or argue ideas, so we can forget exposition and argument. That leaves only narration and description.

Narration is concerned with the action of our stories; it involves energy, pace, and movement. We can write dull, boring narration, or we can write exciting, reader-grabbing narration. So, how do we write exciting narration?

Rule #1: Use Strong Action Verbs

If I write *Bobby was mad,* I'm telling you how Bobby felt. The linking verb (*was*) is not an action verb, so it weakens the sentence . . . If, however, I say, *Bobby slammed the door, threw his books on the floor, and kicked the cat,* I'm using strong action verbs. You see Bobby's actions and conclude, "Boy, Bobby's mad!"

Here are some more examples:

Telling:	*Sue heard a scary noise.*
Showing:	*A noise at the window woke Sue, the scratchy noise of branches—or fingernails.*
Telling:	*A bond of love grew between Mary and her lamb.*
Showing:	*Mary slept in the barn next to Lambie-Pie and fed him from a baby bottle. She buried her face in his woolly coat, and Lambie-Pie licked her face.*

Rule #2—Show, Don't Tell, Emotions

If I write *I'm really tired of the snow,* I've made a statement and you know a fact—I'm tired of snow. But if I write, *If one more stupid snowflake lands in my driveway, I'm going to run away to Tahiti and I'm never coming back,* not only do you know how I feel, you know how intensely I feel it. This is a much more powerful sentence because not only does it intensify the emotion, it also creates an image.

Rule #3—Reveal (show) Characters Through Dialogue or Active Thinking.

Rather than telling the reader a fact through an indirect quote, such as:

> *Last night at dinner Julie was quiet. Finally she told Susie that Herman had dumped her.*

Use action and a direct quote:

> *Susie put the last forkful of fettuccine in her mouth and sighed. "Boy, that was great," she said, "but you haven't eaten a thing, Julie. You haven't said a word either. Are you okay?"*
>
> *"I'm fine. I'm just not hungry."*
>
> *"You don't look fine."*
>
> *"Oh, all right. It's Herman." Julie threw her napkin on the table. "He says we should date other people—just to be sure. But I think he wants out."*

Using dialogue is an excellent way to change from telling to showing:

Telling:	*Bobby told his mother he hated her.*
Showing:	*"I hate you!" Bobby screamed. "You are the wickedest mother in the whole world!"*

Actively showing what a character thinks instead of telling the thought may appear to be a minor change, but it can make a major difference in your writing by putting your readers in your character's head and letting them discover what the character discovers.

Telling:	*Heather thought that the garden was the most beautiful she'd ever seen.*
Showing:	*This is the most beautiful garden I've ever seen, Heather thought.*

Rule #4: Dramatize Flashbacks and Dramatically Narrate Backfill

All fiction (no matter what the length) is made of scenes. Each scene can be classified as either forward action, flashback, or backfill. Forward action moves the story forward. Flashback and backfill are scenes containing previous information that the reader needs to know to completely understand the current situation.

Flashback scenes are so important that we dramatize them so the reader actually lives through the past action with the characters. Backfill scenes provide necessary information which we don't need to dramatize, so we narrate that material. But we must narrate *dramatically*, again by showing the reader through active verbs. Look at this example:

Telling Through Exposition:

Mary's staff never knew what to expect next. One day she was up and the next day she was down. Mary was manic-depressive.

Showing Through Active Narration:

Friday afternoon Mary clinched the Henderson account. To celebrate she treated her entire staff to dinner at the Plaza Room on the 32nd floor of the Chrysler Building. On Saturday at 11 p.m. Mary stood on the ledge of the 32nd floor of the Chrysler Building, screaming "I'm going to jump."

Dramatization:

Actually write out each of these two incidents.

Exposition:	*Mary wanted to kill her husband.*
Narration:	*Mary told me that her goal in life was to kill her husband, Jack, and throw his body to the sharks.*
Dramatization:	*"I'm going to murder that no good, two-timing bastard I married and throw his body to the sharks," Mary commented as she sipped a Mai Tai.*

As fiction writers, we have to decide which scenes to dramatize and which to narrate, but every scene should be *shown* through action and dialogue or through dramatic narration. Showing makes writing active and immediate. The reader feels and experiences what the characters are feeling and experiencing.

Rule #5: Show from the Point of View of Only One Character

Showing is directly related to point of view. If we are firmly entrenched in one character's p.o.v., we will show what that character is doing, thinking, and how she or he is reacting. It is important, however, not to switch point of view within a short story or within a scene of a longer work of fiction. If we're not careful, subtle shifts in p.o.v. can creep into a story. Can you find the subtle p.o.v. shift in this passage which I intend to be from Claudia's point of view?

When Claudia heard the doorbell ring, she gave her platinum curls a pat and undid another button of her gold lamé blouse.

"Good morning, Claudia," Trent said when she opened the door. "Don't you look lovely today. Is this a special occasion?"

"Oh, Trent, you are such a flatterer." Claudia flushed bright red.

The flaw is in the last sentence. Claudia cannot *see herself,* only Trent can see Claudia. By saying she "flushed bright red," we are switching point of view to what Trent can see. We can solve this problem by changing to what Claudia *feels* instead of what she can't see. (*Claudia felt herself flush.*)

Rule # 6: Description Must Be a Function of Character.

Many years ago when I was taking a fiction writing correspondence course, I was called to task for not including any description in my stories. To this day I still have to go through a finished story to decide where I need to add some physical description.

On the other hand, I've read many stories (published and unpublished) which contain long, detailed physical descriptions of the characters and settings that don't add anything to the story. In fact, these descriptions get in the way and detract from the story.

I've always thought there must be a happy medium between these two extremes, and I finally found the answer in *The Elements of Story Telling* by Peter Rubie who says, "*. . . description is a function of viewpoint. It is not the author doing the describing, but the character*"

We usually need much less physical description than we think we need. Physical description of the main character should be limited to a few specific details that help characterize the character. Physical description of other characters should be used only to show how the main character reacts and responds to the other characters.

The purpose of describing physical setting should be limited to concisely presenting the time and place of the story and establishing the mood or atmosphere. Again, *show* how the character reacts and responds to sensory details rather than telling the reader. Read the following two examples. The first contains a lot of description that has no purpose. In the second, the physical description is a function of Stanley, his actions, and reactions.

Example #1

The shrill jangle of the alarm woke Stanley Evans from a sound sleep. He had a headache and his stomach hurt. His eyes fluttered open, and he saw his tuxedo hanging on the closet door. Stan was getting married today, and he had drunk too much at last night's bachelor party. His fiancée, Christine, whom he had known since high school, had told him yesterday not to get drunk. Boy, would she be mad.

Stanley rolled out of his king-size bed with navy blue plaid Ralph Lauren sheets and walked barefooted to the bathroom. The gray Venetian tiles were cold on his size thirteen feet, and he shivered. He ripped open the little foil packet containing two Alka-Seltzer tablets, took them out, and put them into a glass of water. They fizzed loudly and made his headache worse.

Stanley looked in the mirror at his light brown, thinning hair. His usually sparkling brown eyes were dull and bloodshot. His perky smile had left his thin lips. "Boy, I sure look awful!" Stanley said to his reflection. It seemed as though his reflection nodded in agreement.

Stanley drank the Alka-Seltzer as fast as he could. Yuck! It sure tasted awful. Then Stanley took off his blue and white striped pajamas with blue trim around the collar. He turned on the shower. I sure hope this makes me feel better, he thought.

Example #2

The shrill jangle of the alarm brought Stan to an upright position before he'd even opened his eyes. His head throbbed and every muscle in his body ached.

"Oh shit," he muttered wondering if his tongue really was twice its normal size or only felt that way.

Slowly Stan tried to stand, but the room spun. He flopped back on to the bed.

And then like a blow to his already upset stomach Christine's words came back to him. "I know you have to do your male stag party thing," she'd said yesterday, "so get it out of your system. But if you're not at the church sane and sober at two o'clock tomorrow afternoon, the whole thing is off."

"Aw shit," Stan repeated.

Taking a deep breath he stood up, got his bearings, and staggered to the bathroom. He filled a glass with water and plunked in two Alka-Seltzer tablets, then added two more. The unbearably loud fizzing echoed through his head and made his empty stomach even queasier.

With his eyes now partially open, Stan caught a glimpse of some stranger in the mirror. He saw his father's receding hair line, his mother's frown, and alcoholic Grampa Joe's bloodshot eyes. Oh god, he thought, I can't believe when I was eight I was convinced I was adopted.

Stan took another deep breath, chug-a-lugged the now silent morning cocktail, and headed for the shower.

These six **Show; Don't Tell** rules also apply to personal essays, nonfiction, and poetry. In a personal essay we dramatize an anecdote through showing the reader what happened just as we would if we were writing fiction. Use of these rules is what makes dramatic nonfiction alive and exciting.

One of the purposes of poetry is to evoke an emotion through an image, so it's essential to show; don't tell when writing poetry. We can do this by using metaphors rather than similes and by never telling emotions in a poem. Compare the two poems below and see the differences.

The spider is spinning strands of steel
 to catch for her unsuspecting meals.
 a big black fly flies around the hall
Bouncing off the ceiling and walls.
 I feel like I'm that erratic fly
 buzzing crazily around, but not knowing why
 until I drop into the spider's intricate web.
She'll eat me for lunch because I'm dead.

The Web

Undeterred, the spider spins silken cords;
    delicate steel strands that catch for her
        meals of unsuspecting flies.
Her intricate web is strong;
    She is organized, disciplined.
    While the fly, constantly buzzing,
    covers large areas in short periods of time
    accomplishing nothing.
Fly-like,
    I buzz from goal to goal
    bouncing erratically
    off ceiling and walls
    until I drop dazed and weak
    into the web
    a meal for the purposeful spider.

The first is an example of a *telling* poem. The emotions are explained (*"I feel like I'm that erratic fly"*). The second poem uses the metaphor of the spider and the fly to show the narrator's feelings and let the reader draw his own conclusions.

The purpose of all creative writing is to move the reader to feel and experience emotion. This can be done most effectively by showing rather than telling. If you're tired of hearing the show; don't tell rule, try this interpretation by Doug Lipman in his book *The Story Telling Coach.* Doug suggests *don't make a statement; create an image.* That idea jumped out at me because it gives us a definitive way to test our writing. Now we can look at each sentence and ask, "Did I make a statement when I should have created an image?" The answer to that question will tell us when to show and when to tell dramatically.

Because it works: Analyze one of your stories that isn't working. Highlight all the telling passages that make a statement. Work on changing as many as possible to showing passages that create an image. ❊

9

When NOT to Use Description

Years ago when I was taking a fiction correspondence course, one of the assignments was to write a descriptive scene. I didn't do very well on that assignment because I didn't use enough sensory words—colors, smells, sounds, etc. I still have trouble with description. I use very little in a first draft and frequently have to force myself as I rewrite to add a word or two in the proper places. (I can see it in my mind, why can't the reader?)

Too little description is **not** the problem of many of the manuscripts we read, nor is it the problem of many published stories.

Rather than me lecturing you about description, let's play **show; don't tell** and see what you discover. So here's what you do:

A. Read the following story.
B. Then read the rules at the end of the story and use the numbers to refer back to the examples in the story. I have marked at least one example of each "Where NOT to Use Description" rule. You can identify other examples of the same rule. I think you'll quickly recognize the most common description problems.
C. Now read some of your own work, no matter what genre. Put numbers where you have broken any description rules. Then rewrite fixing the broken rules.

The Strange Case of the Smashed, Valuable, Blue and White Wedgwood Vase That Was on the Table in the Foyer [1]
By Glenda Balloch McEwen Baker [1]
Zoë got out of the cab slowly. The sunlight glinted off her honey blonde hair and made her azure blue eyes look like deep forest pools. [3]
"Do you need help with your bundles?" the cab driver asked hopefully. [3]

"No," Zoë answered, "I can get them." She reached into her Gucci purse [6], took out a ten, and gave it to the cab driver.

"Keep the change," she said gleefully. [5]

"Thanks," he replied happily, smiling at the generous tip. Wow, that's some good-looking dame, he thought [3] as she walked sexily up the front steps of her mid-Manhattan, 19th century, brownstone town house, her taupe, leather, two-inch heel pumps clicking on the pavement. [1]

She unlocked the front door and entered the foyer. Immediately she sensed that something was wrong. Snowball, her prize-winning, pure white, long-haired Persian cat, a gift from her great-Aunt Zelda, [1] who usually met her at the door [10], was not rubbing around her slim attractive ankles [6]. Not only that, the blue and white Wedgwood vase that usually sat in the middle of the ball-and-claw-footed mahogany table was lying in smithereens on the Italian marble tile floor.

"Maybe Zack is back," Zoë thought to herself.

As she passed the Baroque, guilt-edged mirror gilt-edged mirror that hung over the mahogany table, she stopped to check her make-up. [2] Her sky blue Donna Karan suit complimented her flawless complexion. Her honey blonde hair glistened, her Estée Lauder painted eyes sparkled. She was perfect. [3]

But why was the vase broken?

Zoë walked determinedly into the living room. She put her five blue and white Bloomingdale bags on the Louis the Nineteenth [8] occasional chair and kicked off her taupe pumps. [6]

"Zachary, where are you?" she called excitedly in her sexy alto voice. She could smell the sweet, cherry-wood pipe tobacco Zack always smoked.

Suddenly a deep resonant voice rang out. "I am not Zachary." A six-foot tall, classically handsome man who looked exactly like Zachary stepped from behind the gold-fringed, deep purple velvet draperies. His eyes darted around in his head to see if they were alone [9].

"Who are you?" Zoë asked in a puzzled tone as their eyes met [9]. "You look exactly like Zachary."

He narrowed his steel gray eyes at her [9]. "Didn't Zack tell you about *me?*" he angrily questioned through gritted, although exceptionally white, teeth.

Zoë sauntered [2] to the purple, pink and mint green floral chintz couch [6] and sat down slowly. "No," she mused [5], "I have no idea who you are, although you do look exactly like Zack."

"I am Zack's identical twin brother Mack," he [5] hissed.

"But he told me you died in an avalanche when you were on a Boy Scout skiing trip at Loon Mountain when you were both at Dartmouth College majoring in sixteenth century British literature [6]," she explained.[5]

"You are wrong!" he shouted loudly [5]. "I majored in fifteenth century Scandinavian literature." He paced across the living room, running his hand through his dark wavy hair. He brought his hand to his forehead, tapped it twice, scratched his left ear, then turned abruptly. [6] "And I did not die in the avalanche," he insisted strongly [5]. "Zack got me lost and then abandoned me in the wilderness." Mack choked back a tear.

"But how did you survive?" Zoë asked politely.

"By my wits," Mack grinned. [5] "But that's another story."

As he took a menacing step toward Zoë, he removed a small, shiny, silver metallic object [1] from his pocket. It was a gun. It was a Walther PK 34 with a silencer. [4 & 8]

Zoë recoiled into the sofa. "What are you going to do?" she asked hysterically.

"I am going to take the one thing that Zack wants most in the world," he emphasized. "I am going to kill you."

Zoë's hand flew to her white, 100% silk, dry-clean only blouse [1 & 2]. "Oh no," she pleaded, "please don't."

Suddenly a shot rang out. Mack slumped to the floor. Zack jumped out from behind the other purple velvet drape. Wisps of misty white smoke drifted from his gun. He bounded across the living room and pulled Zoë into his arms.

"Oh darling I love you so bad." His voice was like honey dripping down a stack of Grandma Brown's golden flapjacks [11]. He kissed her luscious red lips.

A moan shattered the lovers' tranquility. Mack raised his head. "I didn't break your valuable, blue and white Wedgwood vase that was on the table in the foyer," he whispered with his last breath. "It—was—Snowball." Then he died.

Zoë burst into tears.

"Do not concern yourself, my darling," Zack muttered. "He was a no good louse and it was self-defense. Let me kiss your tears away."

"I know that," Zoë quietly affirmed.

"Then why are you crying, my Precious Love," he crooned.

"Whatever shall I do," Zoë sobbed, "about Snowball?"

When NOT to use description

1. When your description is overdone. If you are consistently using two or more adjectives before every noun, you may suffer from **adjective addiction**. The record for the number of adjectives for one noun that I've seen is seven. That's at least four too many. And you probably don't need your entire name for the byline.
2. When your description interrupts the action. Your story should build suspense. Don't interrupt that suspense with (often needless) description.
3. When your description results in a point of view shift. Description must be written through the eyes of the p.o.v. character. The p.o.v. character cannot see his or her own eyes, face, or hair for the most part, so we frequently resort to the old looking-in-the-mirror trick to find a way to get in the description we think we need.
4. When you tell rather than show. If you're using the words **was** or **had,** you are **telling**.

5. When you use tags that have nothing to do with speech. People don't grin or laugh or hiss or sneer words. Another dialogue description problem results from using too many tags and especially tags with adverbs. The results in telling the reader what you want him to know about how the dialogue is being spoken. The emotion should be evident from the dialogue (the words the characters actually speak), not from the tag. This error is very easy to fix because frequently it's just a matter of punctuation.

> Wrong: *"I knew I would catch you," he sneered.*
> Right: *"I knew I would catch you." He sneered.*

On the other hand, if you wrote:
> *"I knew I would catch you," he hissed.*

Would you even consider writing:
> *"I knew I would catch you." He hissed.*

6. When your description (or action) is irrelevant and/or unnecessary.
7. When your description is redundant. By definition shouting is loud; insistence is strong.
8. When the details are incorrect. I don't know anything about guns and I didn't want to take the time to do any research, so I decided just to make up something. It sounds pretty good and nobody will notice. (Oh yes, they will.)
9. When body parts start doing strange things—especially eyes. This is my real pet peeve. Our eyes don't really do anything except sit inside our heads. We can move our eyes back and forth or up and down. And we can roll our eyes. But that's about it, folks. Eyes don't dart or snake or narrow. We can stare (but we can't glue our eyes to anything), we can peek, we can gaze, we can ogle but *we* do those things, *not* our eyes. We can squint, blink, laugh, cry, and flirt, but *we* perform these actions, *not* our eyes. We can lower or shift our gaze (not our eyes), we can lose our sight or correct our vision; again *we* do those seeing-related things, not our eyes. We can cry, we can emit tears, but our eyes don't cry and tears don't squirt from our eyes.
    (Okay, I will concede that eyes can twinkle.)
      We don't perk up our ears to hear and we don't wiggle our noses to smell, so what is all this stuff with eyes?
10. When your description results in unintended humor, usually because of a misplaced modifier or a misplaced phrase. Is it Aunt Zelda who meets Zoë at the door every day? Or Snowball?
11. When your simile or metaphor is inappropriate to the rest of the story.

Yes, description is important. It grounds the reader in time, place, and atmosphere. We show who our characters are by how they look and what they wear. Precise, accurate details bring life to our writing. But we must remember how to use description effectively.

Description must always be relayed through the senses of the point of view character, and it must be a function of action. Which all gets down to that wonderful phrase you've heard a trillion times and don't want to hear again but you're going to—**show; don't tell.**

Here's the Description Test. Ask yourself:

What does this piece of description add to this story?

If the color of her hair and eyes doesn't add anything to the story, maybe it isn't even necessary. You're all aware of the writing sin in which your heroine's eyes are blue on page 17, but they're brown on page 139. As bad an error as this may be, if you're still talking about her eyes on page 139 your story may have more problems than just inconsistent description.

Okay, let's see what we can do to rescue the story of poor Zoë and Zack.

The Strange Case of the Smashed Vase
By Glenda Baker

Zoë got out of the cab slowly.

"Do you need any help with your bundles?" the cab driver asked.

"No," Zoë answered, "I can get them." She gave him a ten. "Keep the change."

"Thanks," he replied, smiling.

Zoë knew she'd over-tipped but today she didn't care. Tonight Zack was returning. She could feel the cabbie watching her as she went up the front steps of her mid-Manhattan town house. She intentionally exaggerated the swing of her hips to give him a thrill.

Zoë unlocked the front door and entered the foyer. Immediately she sensed something was wrong. Snowball was not rubbing around her ankles begging to be fed. Not only that, the blue and white Wedgwood vase that usually sat in the middle of the table lay in smithereens on the floor.

Is Zack back already? Zoë wondered.

As she passed the mirror that hung in the foyer, she stopped to check her make-up. Zack hated if she looked rumpled or unkempt. A quick glance assured her that she looked perfect as usual.

But why was the vase broken?

Zoë went into the living room. She dropped her Bloomingdale bags next to the sofa and kicked off her shoes.

Then she caught the smell of the sweet, cherry-wood pipe tobacco that Zack always smoked. The smell she loved. "Zachary, where are you?" she called.

Suddenly a voice rang out. "I am not Zachary."

A man who looked exactly like Zachary stepped from behind the drapes. He looked quickly around the room. "Are we alone?"

"You look exactly like Zachary," Zoë said. "Who are you?"

He stared at her, his steel eyes cold and piercing, not soft and blue like Zack's eyes. His face went pale with anger. "Didn't Zack tell you about me?"

Cautiously Zoë moved to the sofa. Better not annoy him, she thought. She sat down slowly.

"No," she said, "I have no idea who you are."

"I am Zack's identical twin brother Mack."

"But he told me you died in an avalanche."

"You're wrong!" he shouted. He paced across the living room, then turned abruptly. "I didn't die in the avalanche. Zack got me lost, then abandoned me in the wilderness."

"But how did you survive?"

"By my wits." Mack grinned. "But that's another story."

He stepped closer to Zoë then took a small gun from his pocket. He aimed directly at Zoë's heart.

Zoë cringed. "What are you doing?"

"I am going to take the one thing that Zack wants most in the world." He took another step. "I am going to kill you."

Zoë clutched her throat. "No! Don't!"

Suddenly a shot rang out. Mack slumped to the floor. Zack jumped out from behind the other drape, smoke drifting from his gun. He crossed the living room. "Oh darling, I love you so much." Zack pulled Zoë into his arms and kissed her.

A moan shattered the tranquility. Mack raised his head. "I didn't break your vase," he whispered with his last breath. "It—was—Snowball." Then he died.

Zoë burst into tears.

"Do not concern yourself, my darling," Zack said. "He was a no-good louse and besides it was self-defense."

"I know that, Zack.

"Then why are you crying, my Precious Love?"

"Whatever shall I do," Zoë said between sobs, "about Snowball?"

> The End

Well, maybe some stories aren't worth rescuing after all.

Because it works: Analyze one of your stories by highlighting all the description. Is it necessary? Is it over-done? Does it add to the story or detract from it? Have you created a description dump? Rewrite the story weaving the description throughout the action. ❊

10

The Ten Dialogue Commandments

1. **Dialogue shall have a purpose.** Thou shall not write chit-chat, especially at the beginning and ending of phone conversations and when characters meet or depart, such as:

    "Good morning, Henry."
    "Good morning, Mom."
    "Did you sleep well?"
    "Yes, I did. Thank you for asking."
    "What would you like for breakfast, dear?"
    "I don't have time for breakfast. I'll miss the school bus."
    "But breakfast is the most important meal of the day, Henry."
    "I'll take a banana with me."
    "That's a good idea. Have a good day, son."
    "You too, Mom."
    "Love you."
    "Love you too."
    "Oh by the way, son, I'm leaving your father."

    Get to the point:

    "Good Morning, Mom," Henry said.
    "What's good about it?" Mom slammed the refrigerator door.
    "I just . . ."
    "I'm leaving your father today."
    "You say that every day." Henry grabbed a banana from the counter.
    "Today I mean it," Mom said, as she turned from the refrigerator with a bag of ice chips. Her left eye was black and blue and her lip was bleeding.

2. **Dialogue shall advance the story.** Such as:

> "Who killed Olivia?" Captain Sam Wiley asked.
> "How should I know?" Howard bristled at the question.
> "Because you were the last person to see her alive."

> [Don't stop here—advance the story.]

> "That doesn't mean I killed her."
> "No," Sam continued, "but how do you explain the fact that your fingerprints are on the dagger that was found in her back?"
> "It came from my antique shop. Everything in my shop has my prints on it." Damn, Howard thought, I must have forgotten to wear gloves.

3. **Dialogue shall show character.** What do you know about these two characters from what they say and how they say it?

> "So you think you can outshoot me, you little ne'er-do-well!" Lord Snootface shouted.
> "I didn't really mean that," Timmy said. "What I meant was that . . . I . . . um . . ."
> "Don't give me that drivel. We will duel! Tomorrow at sunrise in the park."
> "Sunrise? But I'm not a morning person."
> "Then I will shoot you dead now and be done with you!"

4. **Thou shall not pack the dialogue** by repeating things the reader already knows, doesn't need to know (soap opera dialogue), or by making the dialogue an information dump.

No soap opera dialogue:
> "As you already know," Hortense began, "I was the last one to see Olivia. I have never liked Olivia since we were in the third grade and she didn't invite me to her birthday party because her mother (the lush), said we were poor and I didn't have a pretty enough dress to wear."

No information dump:
> "Here on the planet Zirax," the alien general began, "we breathe a combination of five molecules of hydrogen and two of ziraxium which makes us all have very high voices and sparkle in the dark like diamonds. The reason we can defy gravity is . . .
> (Three pages later he's still going) ". . . and that is why we'll never be able survive on earth," the general concluded.

5. **Thou shall not write phonetic dialect**, such as:

"Eet ees a nice day, eesn't eet?" Pierre commented.
What does work is:
"It is a nice day, *n'est pas?*" Pierre's French accent made him appear more intelligent than he really was.

6. **Thou shall learn how to punctuate dialogue.**
"Incorrectly punctuated dialogue screams, 'I am an amateur,'" she told us. "An editor will not correct it for you."

Tags can be placed at the beginning, in the middle, or at the end of a line of dialogue. Where it is placed is based on the rhythm and the emphasis you want to create.

 A. He said, "Oh well, it's all over now. I'd better leave."
 B. "Oh well," he said, "it's all over now. I'd better leave."
 C. "Oh well, it's all over now," he said. "I'd better leave."
 D. "Oh well, it's all over now. I'd better leave," he said.

Any of these four examples is correct (if punctuated correctly). I prefer C.

7. **Thou shall make characters' speech sound different**. See #3.

8. **Thou shall use tags as needed and with very few (if any) adverb**s. The emotion shall be in the dialogue, not in the tags as in this example:

"How are you?" Petunia asked lightly.
"Not well," Harvey answered honestly.
"What's wrong?" she inquired seriously.
"I suffer from gout," he pronounced slowly.
"That's too bad," she countered compassionately. "Are you in any pain?"
"My toes throb constantly," he bit out savagely.
"How horrible!" she commented carefully. "What can I do to help?"
"Nothing!" he exploded angrily.
"I am so sorry," she muttered meekly.
"Don't be condescending," he commented coldly.
"I am only concerned that this will affect your performance," she shot back unwisely and a little coyly.
"This will not affect my performance," he gritted bravely, "but I will have to use a cane as I enter the stage."

"Just make sure you do not distract from my performance," she demanded with sudden urgency, then added menacingly, "or you will never set foot on Broadway again."

Keep in mind that "said" is invisible. Many other tags distract from what is being said.

9. **Dialogue shall be appropriate for the character and the era of the story.** Find the error in this one!

"How long will it take to get to Carson City by stagecoach?" Petunia asked. "Like ya know, I've never even been out of Dodge."

10. **Thou shall use only words related to speech as tags.**

"This has been a delightful day," she smiled.
Smiling is not a way of speaking.

"This has been a delightful day." She smiled.

And one more:

11. **Thou shall not write long speeches or too many Dialogue Commandments.**

Writing good dialogue is essential to writing good fiction. Dialogue makes characters come alive, shows who they are, and puts the reader right into the story.
"And remember," she concluded, "what isn't said can be as important as what is."

Because it works: Ask your writing group to help you analyze your dialogue. Assign each character's dialogue to a different person and all of the non-dialogue to another person. Have the group read your dialogue out loud. All you may do is *listen*. Does your dialogue sound natural for each character? Is there too much chitchat? Are there too many tags? Are there places where the readers get confused as to which character is speaking because there aren't enough tags or other indications as to who the speaker is? Then ask the readers how they felt reading their lines. Did it feel natural, forced, or out of character? ❉

11

Write to the Point—of View

Third person limited. Omniscient. First person, past tense. External dramatic. Limited omniscient.

Deciding on point of view is one of the most important decisions you'll make each time you start writing a story. If you've read any articles on point of view, you may have been confused by all the terms. Why so many terms? How can we simplify them so we know what we're talking about?

Part of the problem is that most articles on point of view also talk about tense and person. All the terms get jumbled together. So let's break them down to the basics.

When you start writing fiction, you have to make three decisions. You have to decide:

1. In what tense am I going to tell this story?
2. In what person am I going to tell this story?
3. From which character's point of view am I going to tell this story?

Tense: Tense refers to only one thing: are the verbs going to be in the present tense or the past tense?

Writing in the present tense sounds like this: *Sally wakes up in a strange bed. She doesn't know where she is. How did I get here? she wonders. "Is anyone here?" she calls out.*

The only other possibility is past tense: *Sally woke up in a strange bed. She didn't know where she was. How did I get here? she wondered. "Is anyone here?" she called out.*

While the past tense is often most comfortable to write in, the present tense gives a feeling of immediacy. The reader experiences events as the character does. The past tense puts a little distance between the reader and the character.

Person: Your second decision is which person to write the story in. You have only three choices: first person, second person, or third person. These are grammatical terms used to designate whether the subject of the sentence is speaking, being spoken to, or being spoken about.

Using the first person, the subject of the sentence is the person speaking; it is an "I/we" story: *I woke up in a strange bed. I didn't know where I was. How did I get here? I wondered. "Is anyone here?" I called out.*

This example was written in the first person and in past tense. It could also be written in the first person present tense: *I wake up in a strange bed. I don't know where I am. How did I get here? I wonder. "Is anyone here?" I call out.*

To successfully write in the first person, you must closely identify with the character. You must see, taste, hear, and know what the character is thinking and feeling. This is also the limitation of writing in the first person: You can present only information that your main character knows.

Using the **second person**, the subject of the sentence is being spoken to. It is a "you" story which, if written in the present tense, sounds like this: *You wake up in a strange bed. You don't know where you are. How did you get here? you wonder. "Is anyone here?" you call out.*

The same thing may also be written in the past tense: *You woke up in a strange bed. You didn't know where you were. How did you get here? you wondered. "Is anyone here?" you called out.*

I'm not sure what the advantages of writing in the second person are. It's not easy to write or read. Although entire books or large portions of books are written in the second person such as *Half Asleep in Frog Pajamas* by Tom Robbins and *Bright Lights, Big City* by Jay McInerney, I think second person works better for shorter pieces. The intent is to make you, the reader, experience the events as if they were happening to you.

Your third option is the third person in which the subject is being spoken about. This is a "he/she" story, and again may be written in either the present or the past tense: *Sally wakes up in a strange bed. She wonders where she is. How did I get here? she wonders. "Is anyone here?" she calls out.* (Present tense.)

Sally woke up in a strange bed. She wondered where she was. How did I get here? she wondered. "Is anyone here?" she called out. (Past tense.)

This is probably the most common and most natural way of writing, but it's also easier to switch points of view when writing in the third person, i.e. inadvertently get into other characters' heads.

Point of View: Your third decision is: From which character's point of view am I going to tell this story? Which character's head am I going to get into? Which character's thoughts and feelings am I going to record?

Here again you have only three options: 1) the point of view of a single character, 2) point of view of more than one character, or 3) just report actions and reactions and not get into any character's head.

Let's say your short story has three characters in it, Fluffy, Muffy, and Buffy. Here are your options: You can tell the story as 1) Fluffy sees, hears, feels, and understands it; as Muffy sees, hears, feels, and understands it; as Buffy sees, hears, feels, and understands it; 2) from all their points of view; or 3) from none of their points of view.

How do you decide which to use?

First, it depends on what you are writing. If you are writing a short story, stick with one point of view. A short story focuses on a single story line, the dramatization of events (frequently a single event) leading to a single outcome. Because it is short in length, you don't have time to fully develop more than one character. Decide which character knows the most about the story. Write the story through the eyes, feelings, and thoughts of that character. Do not switch to the thoughts and feelings of any other character.

If you are writing a novel, you often need to use more than one point of view because one character doesn't know everything that is going on with all the other characters. My advice here is not to change point of view within a scene. Make clear transitions from one point of view character to the next at either a section or a chapter break so the reader doesn't become confused.

Second, your p.o.v. character depends on which character knows the most about the story. If Fluffy knows all the details, write the story from Fluffy's p.o.v. But if Muffy or Buffy know more, write the story from either of their points of view.

You may have to experiment to decide which p.o.v. to use. Fluffy's p.o.v. may be working fine. Then you get to something that happens to Muffy that Fluffy doesn't know about. How can you write this scene without switching to Muffy's p.o.v.? Muffy could tell Fluffy what happened. Someone else could tell Fluffy what happened. Or maybe Muffy knows more about the story and the whole thing should be written from her p.o.v. You'll have to experiment and see what works best.

Objective or External Dramatic: This point of view needs a few word of its own. The objective p.o.v. may be the hardest of all to write. Here the writer reports only what the main characters do and say. The writer does not get into any character's head so cannot report what any character tastes, smells, feels tactilely or emotionally. Report only actions and reactions and dialogue. There are no judgments or comments by the writer. It is the ultimate *show, don't tell story*. This cannot be a first person story.

In the objective p.o.v. Sally can't "wonder"; she can't "think." Even words like "strange" are judgment calls on the part of the writer. So we are left with:

Sally woke up in a bed in a hotel room. "Is anyone here?" she called out.

We could add:

She picked up the phone. "Where am I?" she asked the concierge. "What hotel is this?"

Point of view may also be defined as perspective; each character has a different perspective as to what actually happened.

Have you ever been at a family get together where Uncle Bill says, "Remember the time Aunt Lydia fell in the lake?" and then he launches into a detailed account of what happened. He may be only a few sentences into his story when Cousin Emily interrupts and says, "No, Bill, that isn't the way it happened at all!" then she starts telling her version. Before the story is done several other family members have added what they remember. Each story may be quite different from the others. And Aunt Lydia? She doesn't remember it at all. She says it must have happened to her sister Gertrude. Four different points of view; four different stories.

Another example is to listen to the story of each eyewitness to a crime. One says that the getaway car was dark blue, another says it was dark green, the third is convinced it was black. One says the robber was a tall, thin redhead; another says he was of medium build and had brown hair; the third says he was sure it was a short, blonde woman dressed in combat fatigues. More than one successful mystery story has been based on the faulty evidence of the "eyewitness."

That's what point of view is all about. Each character sees the events in his or her own time frame, location, and from a particular mind set. So if you write your story from Fluffy's p.o.v. and then decide to rewrite it from Muffy's p.o.v., you may find that you come out with a completely different story. Then you have to decide which works best.

A great point of view exercise is to take a familiar fairy tale (Cinderella or Little Red Riding Hood) and rewrite it strictly from the p.o.v. of some character other than the one usually considered the main character. Cinderella may be the main character, but how did one of her stepsisters perceive the ball and the search for the owner of the glass slipper? How did the Fairy Godmother see it? Or Prince Charming?

We all know the details of Little Red Riding Hood, but tell the story from the wolf's p.o.v. (he was probably just an innocent victim) or from Grandmother's.

Main Character/Point of View Character: One thing to keep in mind is that the point of view character may not necessarily be the main character. The p.o.v. character might be a narrator who watches what happens to the main character. One of the best examples of a narrator p.o.v. character is *Moby Dick*, where Captain Ahab is the main character but the story is told through the eyes of Ishmael. Another is the Sherlock Holmes stories narrated by p.o.v. character Dr. Watson.

Point of View Shift—Shifts in p.o.v. can easily sneak into your story if you are not careful. Let's go back to Sally waking up in the strange bed:

Sally wakes up in a strange bed. She doesn't know where she is. How did I get here? she wonders "Is anyone here?" she calls out.

The hotel room is deathly quiet. No one is there. Sally picks up the phone and dials the front desk. "Can you tell me where I am?" she asks the concierge.

My, this woman sounds scared, the concierge thinks.

Did you catch it? As soon as you write what the concierge thinks, you are in his head and are now writing from his p.o.v. Some p.o.v. shifts are more subtle.

Suddenly Sally remembered! Gregg! Last night her boss Gregg had invited her out for a drink. After several drinks, Sally had told Gregg, married Gregg, that she'd always had a crush on him. Oh no! What had she done? Sally blushed bright red.

Did you catch that one? Sally blushing bright red is a point of view shift because Sally can't see herself blush. Somebody else would have to see her and report that she was blushing bright red. Sally can feel herself blush, but she can't see it.

"Now you're getting picky," you're saying. And my answer is, "Yes, I am." Shifts in p.o.v. can be subtle, but they jar readers and editors.

When I started writing the novella I've just finished, I knew it was going to be a first person story. But for some unknown reason, I started writing it in the present tense. Every time I sat down to write more of the first draft, I would write in the present tense for awhile. At some point I'd shift into the past tense. After another few hundred words I'd realize what I'd done, then go back and change all the past tense verbs to present tense. After about 7,000 words of this silliness, I asked myself, "Why are you writing this in the present tense?" I didn't have any good answer and realized the whole story would work better in the past tense. It was a job changing all the verbs back to past tense (no computer program for that!), but it was much easier to make the change after 7,000 words than after 20,000.

On the other hand, Jim, a member of my writing group wrote a story in the past tense (again a first person story) and even won a prize for it. Some time later he decided that the story would really work better in the present tense. He made the change and is much happier with the result.

Like other elements of fiction (such as characterization, dialogue, and description), tense, person, and point of view are tools. Your job is to decide which tool will get the job done most effectively. If your story isn't working, take a minute to consider if a change in tense, person, or point of view character would solve the problem.

Because it works:

1. Take a short scene from a story you have written from the point of view of one character and write it from the point of view of the other character. How does the story change?

2. Write a well-known fairy tale from the p.o.v. of one of the characters not generally thought of as the main character, i.e. the wolf in "Little Red Riding Hood" or the witch in "Hansel and Gretel."

3. Use the following situation:
    The setting: a restaurant at which a wedding rehearsal dinner is being held.
    Characters: the entire wedding party is at the dinner. Some of these people are the bride, the groom, the maid of honor, the best man, and the bride's mother.
    The situation: sometime during the evening the groom goes into the lobby. A woman who is not part of the wedding rehearsal guests approaches the groom. They talk and then they kiss. The woman leaves and the groom returns to the party.
    The conflict: unknown to the groom, one other person witnessed the groom talking to and kissing the other woman. This character then confronts the groom.
    The assignment: write two first person accounts of this story, one from the point of view of the groom and one from the point of view of the witness.

First, you have to decide who the other woman is and why she's there kissing the groom.

Next, decide which character witnessed the incident and is going to confront the groom.

Then, get into the skin and the mind of the characters you write about. What did the witness actually see?

How does he or she interpret the situation?

How does this character feel physically? Emotionally?

How does the groom feel about this situation? How does he respond when confronted by the witness?

Resolve the conflict. ✵

12

More Points on Point of View

Since I wrote "Write to the Point—of View" I've had some additional thoughts on the subject and I've received some letters on my article which I'd like to share.

First my thoughts:

Nothing is carved in stone. Guidelines are just that—guidelines. For every guideline, suggestion, or bit of advice any editor offers, you can show me examples of authors (famous authors) who have done just the opposite.

Editors have their own particular peeves. One of mine is p.o.v. shifts. To me they are, at the least, jarring; at the worst, I feel the writer does not know whose story she's writing. I believe a short story should be written from only one p.o.v. In "The Short Happy Life of Francis Macomber," however, Ernest Hemingway is in the heads of four characters including that of the lion in the story. I'm pretty sure Ernest had reasons for doing it—whether it's jarring to me or not.

Think of p.o.v. as a continuum. At one end is the omniscient p.o.v., i.e. author is in every character's head, reporting every character's thoughts, feelings, and reactions. It can be done. It has been done. Maybe you'd like to do it.

At the opposite end of the line is the objective p.o.v. (sometimes called external dramatic) in which the author does not get into any character's head. She reports only actions and reactions. It can be done. It has been done. Maybe you'd like to write from the external dramatic p.o.v.

In between these two extremes on our p.o.v. continuum are two choices: should you write from one point of view or more than one? If you choose one, which one? If you choose more than one, then you need to decide how many points of view and how to keep the reader clear as to whose p.o.v. you're currently using.

It can be done. They've all been done. Just know what you're doing and why you're doing it.

There is, however, a difference between consciously using multiple points of view and unknowingly jumping in and out of heads.

For example, some time ago we received an excellent novel excerpt. The story was written consistently from the p.o.v. of a young mother who was a runaway slave. About two-thirds of the way through the excerpt, the woman went to a marketplace to buy some food. At that point there was a sentence something like: *What a lovely young woman, the baker thought.*

This is a jarring p.o.v. shift that, I'm sure, was written unconsciously. We called it to the author's attention, she fixed it, and we published her excellent novel excerpt.

Arline Chase from Cambridge, Maryland writes: *I've just read your article on point-of-view. WOW. Clear, concise, to the point, and in no way confusing. Would that I read it 20 years ago! I wouldn't have spent years dancing around with the p.o.v. bear at the writer's picnic.*

I know some people, even some well-published and big name writers, who ignore the p.o.v. rules. That makes it very hard for students to understand when you explain the rules to them, because they come back with, "Haven't you read Ms. Famous A. Successful-Writer? Because she does it my way all the time." But I have heard senior editors from major hardcover publishing houses say that slipping p.o.v. is "sloppy and unprofessional" and also a "big turn off." Ms. Famous A. may get away with it, because the company is making a Whole Lot of Money from her books and essentially, she can do anything she wants to. But those of us who are not yet producing millions for anyone can't afford to be less than professional, especially these days, when the market is so tight.

Again, this is the best and easiest explanation I've seen. As you know, I'm an instructor for Writer's Digest School. Would you mind if I made copies of the article to share with some of my students who are having problems with that aspect of short story writing?

R. W. of Massachusetts writes: *Thank you so much for an excellent article in the last issue. It was clearly written and very informative and many will surely benefit from your words of wisdom.*

In the light of your advice, I returned to several of my writings and focused on the point-of-view aspect. I rewrote selected passages numerous times as you suggested, but in most cases I preferred my original versions despite the fact that they appeared to contradict your guidelines.

Great! As a result of my article, R. has done some thinking and some experimenting. Now she's consciously aware of what she did and why she did it. I challenge you all to do the same thing.

R. then comments that several people who have read her novel, including a literary agent, didn't comment on the p.o.v. question. Then either it's not their pet peeve or it isn't an issue because R. may have handled it correctly.

R. writes: *I would therefore proffer that it is possible to write from more than one point of view in a short story, providing the switches are necessary and not casual or careless, and providing they are obvious.*

Exactly.

She also comments that my guideline of writing a short story from only one p.o.v. is restrictive. I agree. And that's why writing short stories is such a challenge. To quote Nancy Kress from *Beginnings, Middles & Endings*, "The shorter the piece of fiction, the more skillful you must be . . . That's why there are more good novelists than good short story writers."

Nancy Kress says that if you do choose to write from multiple points of view (and again this article deals with novels), "A prime concern should be minimizing the fragmentation. If a reader is bounced from one head to another every few sentences, she's going to get motion sickness."

I tell my students that I don't make the rules; I just enforce them. I also tell them they have to know the rules before they can break them. Experimenting is one of the exciting aspects of writing and rewriting. But keep in mind that when you take a p.o.v. risk, you might get caught by an editor who finds point of view shifts jarring.

Because it works: Analyze one of your stories that isn't working. Try changing the p.o.v. character. Does the story work better? Also analyze stories that do work. Can you find any p.o.v. shifts—even very subtle ones? Rewrite removing p.o.v. shifts. ❀

13

The Eight Awful Endings

Pretend you're an editor. You have twenty-five manuscripts to read. You go through the first fifteen pretty quickly because the beginnings are so boring not one of them grabs you, so you don't read beyond page two. (You are not an *NEWN* editor, because we do read every submission.)

By now you are very discouraged.

Then you pick up manuscript #16, and before you know it you're on page 7. This is an exciting story with interesting characters! You are caught up in the conflict, eager to turn the page to see what happens next. The tension is building. How will John Q. Hero solve his problem?

You reach the last page. The last paragraph. The last sentence.

"No! No! No!" you scream. "You can't do that!"

Another disappointing ending. Another rejected story. Another editor banging her head on her desk.

As horrible as a bad beginning is, to an editor who has invested her time and her hopes in a story, a bad ending is even worse.

What do I mean by a bad ending? Here are examples of *The Eight Awful Endings:*

1. **It Was All a Dream**: Of all the bad endings, this is the worst. Everything that happened in the story was a dream. I call it the Dallas Ending. For those of you old enough to remember the TV series *Dallas*, a major decision (removing Bobby Ewing from the show for an entire season and then deciding to have him return) was explained away by having his wife Pam wake up one morning a year later, hear the shower running, out comes Bobby (who we haven't seen for the entire season), and Pam says, "Oh Bobby, I had the strangest dream!" For a year? Even non-writer viewers didn't buy that one.

2. **Deus Ex Machina**: The term *deus ex machina* (god from a machine) comes from Greek drama in which the playwright got the characters into such a mess that he

couldn't figure out how to solve it. So he had a god (*deus*) come down from (*ex*) Mount Olympus in a chariot (*machina*) to make everything right again.

The contemporary *deus ex machina* ending is again a result of the writer getting the characters into complications so horrendous that s/he can't figure out how to solve the problems. So s/he resorts to the villain dropping dead of a convenient heart attack when he had no previous history of coronary problems. Or it's the U.S. Cavalry to the rescue, when last we knew the soldiers were five hundred miles away.

When your character gets into problems, he has to get himself out by using his wits. If he's going to have a heart attack, you have to let the reader know earlier in the story that this man has a heart problem.

3. **Moment of Truth Out of the Blue:** After page upon page of Dad verbally abusing his family, little Johnnie takes him aside one day and says, *"Please don't say those bad things to us anymore; it hurts our feelings."* And then Dad says, *"Oh, silly, me. You are right. I will never say bad things again."* End of story.

   The resolution of a story must be in proportion to the degree of the conflict. If Dad's brother-in-law discovers what an s.o.b. Dad is and says, *"You do this anymore and I'll punch your lights out for good,"* then Dad might have a moment of enlightenment that changes his attitude.

4. **Let the Reader Figure It Out For Himself:** After pages and pages of Ernestine's harrowing problems, the story ends with: *"Ernestine walked confidently into the sunset now knowing exactly what she had to do."* The End.

   Not fair! "The Lady or the Tiger" notwithstanding, the writer has to give the reader at least a hint as to what Ernestine is going to do. *"Ernestine walked confidently to the edge of the Grand Canyon, laid her purse on a convenient rock, and jumped."* Or *"Ernestine walked confidently onto the plane bound for Hawaii—and freedom."* With only a few more words, the reader knows what Ernestine is going to do.

5. **The Surprise Ending:** Here we have the engrossing perils of two star-crossed lovers, only to be told in the last sentence that Susie is a schnauzer and Daniel is a Dalmatian. (Don't laugh; it's been done.) A surprise ending isn't a bad technique. It should, however, leave the reader saying, "I should have seen that coming!"—not, "Where the heck did that come from?"

   A good surprise ending involves casual foreshadowing and planting clues throughout the story so that the surprise ending makes sense.

6. **The Fade to Black or Soap Opera Ending:** The last lines of the story are:

   Petunia opened the door. A tall, handsome man stood on the porch. "Are you Petunia Gardner?" he asked.

   "Yes, I am."

   "I am Horace, the son you gave up for adoption when I was born."

   The End

   This ending is incomplete because we have just witnessed major action but we don't see any *reaction* from Petunia. This works (maybe) in soap operas because soap producers know they have you hooked and you'll tune in tomorrow to see Petunia's reaction. But it doesn't work for the ending of a short story. Readers want to know what Petunia felt and did after receiving this startling news.

7. **Too Long, Too Drawn-Out Ending:** The story ends but the writing doesn't.

> *"I hate you, Ian, and I never want to see you again." Hortense slammed the door barring Ian from the house forever. It was over—finally.*
>
> *Hortense went into the kitchen and made herself a cup of tea. She liked sugar in her tea and a touch of lemon if she had some. She drank the tea, read the newspaper, fed her cat, and then went to bed. The End.*

I don't think I have to explain that one. The story ends when the dramatic action ends.

8. **The Rushed Ending:** Here the writer runs out of energy or suddenly becomes aware that s/he's written 1,475 words and the maximum for the assignment or contest is 1,500 words. The writer summarizes the end by telling what happened instead of showing (dramatizing) the ending event.

> *(1,489 words) "And so Josephine decided to jump off (1,496) the nearest (1,497) bridge (1,499)." The End* [Whew, I just made it with just one word to spare!]

If readers have followed Josephine through all her trials and tribulations, they deserve a little more drama as she teeters on the rail ready to let go. And as for not going over the word length of the story, a better suggestion would be to do major editing throughout the entire piece to remove all unnecessary words.

Don't ruin your story by resorting to any of these **Eight Awful Endings**. Think your ending through. Does it satisfy the reader? Will it prevent an editor from a self-inflicted brain concussion from banging her head on her desk? I hope so.

Because it works: Read several of your stories to see if you are guilty of using any of the Eight Awful Endings. Change Awful Endings to Satisfying Endings that resolve the conflict. ✤

THE WRITING PROCESS—
BECAUSE IT WORKS

14

Can Writing Be Taught?

I've read several books on fiction writing. Inevitably the question "Can writing be taught?" is raised. The answers vary from "yes" to "no" to "maybe."

Before I tell you which of those answers I agree with, let's think about this question.

First of all, writers (as well as dancers, artists, musicians, athletes, engineers, psychiatrists, etc., etc., etc.) are not born. Only babies are born. No doctor ever said, "Congratulations, Mrs. Jones! You've given birth to a seven-pound-eight-ounce writer!" So somewhere along the line some of us learned to write while others learned to be artists, athletes, and engineers.

When I teach Basic Composition, I teach grammar, punctuation, and usage. I teach students how to write a narration paper, a definition paper, a comparison and contrast paper. I have also taught how to write nonfiction articles and how to write poetry (all about rhyme and rhythm, simile and metaphor, free verse and structured poems). I have also conducted creativity workshops: instructed students how use the techniques of brainstorming, clustering, and free writing.

When I teach short fiction writing, I teach how to handle character and setting, the difference between a situation and a story, the elements of effective dialogue, good and bad beginnings, good and bad endings, and everything in between.

Has my teaching been successful? Definitely **yes** and definitely **no.** I've had students whose first attempts at fiction resulted in prize-winning stories. But I've also had basic composition students who after ten weeks of classes still struggle to write three complete sentences. And again, everything in between. I've had students who didn't want the ten-week course to end, and I've had students who came the first night never to return again.

Two students are taught the same material by the same teacher: one becomes a prize winning writer; the other still struggles to put words on paper. So what's the difference? The first answer that comes to mind may very well be: the students are different.

Yes!

But now we have to ask a different question. The question is not can writing be taught, but can writing be learned?

And the answer to that is a definite **maybe.**

As in any art, sport, or discipline, a good teacher can teach basic concepts. Some students will grasp them; others won't. Why?

Because some students have the innate skills needed, i.e. verbal skills for writing, visual skills for art, auditory skills for music, or physical skills for sports. Other students don't have those skills, and never will.

For example, I grew up in New Hampshire about ten miles from Mount Gunstock—smack dab in the middle of ski country. One afternoon a week all winter long, the grammar school students were taken to the slopes so we could *learn to ski.* I hated every minute of it, and I never could "get it".

As a child, my dream was to join the Ice Capades. The only problem was that I couldn't skate. I still can't. With the exception of archery, I hated gym class from grammar school through college. A number of years ago (in a moment of weakness) I decided to take an aerobics class. After eight weeks of repeating the same routines, I still couldn't keep in step with everybody else and was always going left when everybody else was going right. Or was it the other way around? Do you notice a pattern here? I have no innate physical skills. (Well, I can walk and chew gum at the same time, but even that takes concentration.)

And some of my students, students who truly want to develop their writing skills, have very low levels of innate verbal skills. No matter how hard they try, writing will never come easily to them. They are, however, excellent carpenters, mechanics, baseball players, dressmakers, or childcare workers.

I have also had students who "get" the mechanics of writing, but for some reason have a very difficult time with the imaginative, creative side of writing. They very often struggle with fiction but may be excellent nonfiction writers.

If you are struggling with some aspect of your writing career, the career that supports you, or if you have children in school who are not doing well academically, I highly recommend you read *Seven Kinds of Smart* by Thomas Armstrong (Plume—Penguin Group, 1993). You may learn something about yourself or your child. You may learn that you have been struggling in some areas because you lack the basic skills needed for that endeavor. And just as importantly, you may learn where your strengths do lie. Finding their natural abilities is extremely important for children who are struggling with an academic subject.

So I close with my original question: Can writing be taught? And with my original answer: Yes, no, and maybe.

Because it works: Think about people you know who struggle with writing. What activities can they do easily and well? ❋

15

Does Spelling Count?

For about ten years I taught a basic composition course through a local adult education program. Over a hundred students from a wide variety of backgrounds and proficiency levels took my ten-week course either to improve their writing skills for their jobs or because they aspired to a writing career. But no matter why they took the course, 95% of my students made the same errors in their writing.

When I became an editor of *NEWN*, I was surprised to see the same errors in many of the submissions that come across my desk from professional writers. (If you submit material to any publication to be published for payment or copies, you are a professional writer. Professionalism is a matter of intent and attitude, not how much you earn.)

We all want our stories and articles to be accepted by the editors we send them to. Occasional grammar, spelling, punctuation, and other errors shouldn't strongly influence an editor's opinion of your work. But if an editor has to make a choice between a piece full of errors and one with few or none, the hard truth is that the editor can't help but be biased in favor of the less flawed piece.

Here are the most common errors I see. Remove these from your work, so any editor will look more favorably on your submissions.

1. **COMMA PROBLEMS:** The biggest problem I see is *commas where they shouldn't be; no commas where they should be.* If you haven't reviewed punctuation since high school (or junior high), a refresher course may be in order. Here's a quick and partial review:

   A. You *must* put a comma before the conjunction that joins the two independent clauses of a compound sentence.
      We went to the theater, but the show had been canceled.

B.   An introductory dependent clause must be set off by a comma. A dependent clause that follows the independent clause is *not* set off by a comma.

> *When we got to the theater, we were told that the show had been canceled.*
>
> *We were told that the show had been canceled when we got to the theater.*

C.   Put a comma between each element in a list *and* before the conjunction.

> *We ate hot dogs, hamburgers, pickles, and chips.*
>
> *Take the potatoes home, wash them, peel them, and boil them.*

D.   When two verbs joined by a conjunction apply to the same subject, *do not* put a comma before the conjunction.

> *Sally completed all her courses and graduated with honors.* (No comma after *courses*.)

2.   **INCOMPLETE SENTENCES:** Any group of words starting with a subordinating conjunction (such as *while, although, after, during,* etc.) is a dependent clause and should not be presented as a complete sentence.

Incorrect: *She was happy school was over. Although she'd miss her friends during the summer.*
Correct: *She was happy school was over although she'd miss her friends during the summer.*
Correct: *Although she'd miss her friends during the summer, she was happy school was over.*

Incomplete sentences may be used effectively in dialogue and as the thoughts of characters. Editors know when you're using this technique correctly; they also know when you don't know the rules of grammar and punctuation.

3.   **CAPITALIZATION OF PROPER NOUNS**: Any name on a box, a bottle, a package, (e.g. any brand or registered trademark) must be capitalized. The problem is that the names of some product are used so commonly that we forget they are trademarks. Example:

I need a tissue. (Tissue is a generic term and doesn't need to be capitalized.)
I need a Kleenex. (Kleenex is a registered trademark and must be capitalized.)

This is not a suggestion. Writers can get into major trouble if they do not acknowledge product trademarks. All you have to do is capitalize the name.

4.   **USAGE:** English is a fascinating language. We have so many words that sound the same but are spelled differently and have very different meanings. For example, *to, too,* and *two; your* and *you're; its* and *it's.* These are only a few; there are many, many more. And because they are legitimate words, your computer spell check program will not catch the incorrect use of these words. You need to know which word in these many confusing pairs and trios is correct for the sentence you're (not: *your!*) writing.

I also see many spellings that aren't legitimate. There is no such word as *alot;* it is always *a lot.* It's *through,* not *thru.* Never use abbreviated spelling *(lite, nite)* unless the word is part of a brand name.

Do you know that *alright* is not an acceptable word? It should always be *all right. All ready* and *already* are both legitimate, but when do you use which?

No writer's library is complete without a style manual which will answer these grammar, punctuation, and usage questions. I recommend the paperback, spiral bound edition of *The Gregg Reference Manual* published by McGraw-Hill.

5.   **THERE** is a useless word. Get rid of it!
We went on a picnic. There were ants everywhere.
We went on a picnic. Ants were everywhere.

We stayed at a quaint country inn. There were candles in every window.
We stayed at a quaint country inn. Candles decorated every window.

6.   **USE OF WEAK VERBS WITH TOO MANY ADVERBS**. Why write:
Jeff walked slowly down the street when you could write:
Jeff meandered down the street. (Or wandered or staggered or swaggered or any of twenty other words.)

Each has its own subtle connotation to show the exact meaning you want to convey.

7.   **ACTIVE OR PASSIVE VOICE:** One of the hardest things for students of English grammar to keep straight is when to use the *active voice* and when to use the *passive voice.* Maybe you've forgotten what these terms mean and when to use them. In the sentence:
The lady across the street raises roses.
The subject (lady) is performing the action, so the sentence is said to be in the active voice—the subject *performs the action.*
In the sentence:
Roses are raised by the lady across the street.
The subject (roses) is receiving the action, so the sentence is said to be in the passive voice—the subject *receives the action.*

The active voice is usually better because it is *emphatic and direct.* The passive voice is weaker, but there definitely is a place for it. The passive voice should be used when the *doer* is unknown or unimportant. The use of the active voice in the following sentence results in a vague sentence.
We went to a county fair. They were selling apple cider.
Who was selling the cider? Who are *they?* Does it even matter who's selling the cider? If the answer is *no* or *we don't know,* this is the place for the passive voice—what's important is that cider was being sold.

We went to a county fair. Apple cider was being sold.
Use the active voice most of the time.
Use the passive voice: When the action of the verb is more important than the doer, when the doer is unknown, or when you wish to emphasize the *receiver* of the action rather than the doer.

8. **WORDINESS:** You can often cut several words from your sentences and/or combine several sentences into one making your writing less wordy and more concise.

Wordy: *Decide on the pattern and spacing between tiles which you would like.*
Less Wordy: *Plan the tile pattern and spacing.*
Wordy: *I have combined two recipes. One is for the dough. The other is for the topping.*
Less Wordy: *I have combined a dough recipe with a topping recipe.*

As the title of Gary Provost's book says, *"Make Every Word Count!"*

9. **NUMBERS:** Words vs. Figures
Rule #1: Compound numbers are always hyphenated when written as words: *twenty-five, thirty-seven, ninety-nine.*
Rule #2: When a number is two words or one hyphenated word, write it in words.
    We expected one hundred people but only seventy-five came.
Rule #3: When a number is more than two words or longer than one hyphenated word, write it in *figures.* Hence,
    Mavis wants to lose twenty-five pounds. (One hyphenated word: write the words)
    Mavis weighs 137 *pounds.* (four words: write the figure)
Rule #4: Never start a sentence with a figure; always use the words no matter how many words it is.

Writing is much more than grammar, spelling, punctuation, and usage. But they *all* do count. A manuscript full of these mechanical errors is like spinach in your teeth, gravy on your tie, or a run in your stocking. An occasional accident can be forgiven; but when they dot your manuscript like confetti, an editor says, "If this writer doesn't care about his writing, neither do I."

Because it works: Make sure you have a current dictionary and style manual (such as *The Gregg Reference Manual* or *The New York Times* or *Chicago* manuals), so you'll have answers to your spelling and grammar questions when you need them.
Make use of writer friends by exchanging manuscripts for proof reading. A different set of eyes can find typos or other errors that you don't see.
Also make use of your spell and grammar checker to spot errors you might have missed. ✤

16

De-Mystify Your Writing Process

My muse visited me on Sunday, March 11, 2001, during my early morning shower—she always comes to me early in the morning. She made me think of the silly velvet Elvis painting that hangs in my basement. I thought about that image all morning while I took care of my stay-at-home-mom duties of dirty diapers, laundry, and dishwashing.

My best writing surge over the play idea that developed was on April 1st when I got an entire four hours to myself to write. I work best when I have a big chunk of time to devote to the project. My motivation slowed by May 3rd, when a month of birthdays, family events, home improvements, and two-year-old behavior prevented me from focusing on my writing. I resolved the problem by accepting the fact that then was not the time to work on that particular project. I kept motivated because I knew when life slowed down, my project would be ready and waiting and I'd have a fresh new perspective on it.

How do I know all this? Because I keep a project journal. I'm not talking about the mini-spiral notebook that I keep in my purse or on my nightstand in which I jot down ideas, bits of dialogue, character descriptions, or interesting facts. I'm talking about a file on my computer the sole purpose of which is to track the journey of my play. Let's face it, writing is a process not a result. Sure, most writers start writing because they want to be paid for their writing. But such a goal will keep a writer motivated only through so many blocks and obstacles. And such a goal limits the writer from seeing the big picture, the journey from first idea to finished project: the development of story and writer.

There are two main reasons why you should keep a project journal. First, the more you know about your process, the easier writing will be for you. If you know that you get your best ideas right before you fall asleep at night, you can be prepared to jot them down then. If you know that a mundane task like mowing the lawn allows you to have some quiet time to think about your story, you can feel good about doing that rather than staring at a blank page. If you know you work best for the two hours before everyone in the house wakes up, you'll be able to use your time most wisely. Getting one hour of focused work done each day is better than sitting at a computer for eight hours a day because you think that's what a professional writer should do.

Second, by keeping a project journal you'll realize that you work on your writing more than just the time that you spend typing or writing. Hours and hours of thoughts inhabit your mind. The times you talk to your writer friends about an idea. The times when you see someone at the grocery store who has all the characteristics you need in your villain. The times while you change diapers, wash dishes, fold laundry or any other mundane task when your mind molds, shapes, and reshapes your idea. All of that needs to be documented.

Each project deserves its own journal. Even if you are like me and work on several projects at a time, give each project its own journal. Write in the journal only when you have thought about, done some writing on, or in some other way worked on that particular project. (Note: this means you probably won't write in the project journal every day and that's okay). Include daily life trivialities only if they add to the project itself (after slicing your finger while cutting apples, you discover the easiest way to get blood out of silk which will help the lead character in your murder mystery). Or if it directly relates to your writing process (you learn that you cannot focus on writing when your son is watching *Between the Lions* because it's much too entertaining for you too). Write concisely and to the point. Don't bother with correct spelling, grammar, complete sentences, or any of the other things that editors care about. This journal is for you and you alone. Type in green capital letters if it makes you feel good. Write it in a spiral notebook with a purple marker if you prefer. It doesn't matter. Just take the time to keep the journal.

To help you get started, here are some excerpts from my project journal regarding my current, as yet untitled, one-act play. Notice the depth of information, yet the concise writing style. (Please note: these are not consecutive entries):

Sunday, March 11, 2001:
While in the shower this morning at 6 a.m., I began thinking of that silly Elvis on black velvet that hangs in the basement. Suddenly saw humorous scene: two characters, man and a woman who are breaking up, fighting over that stupid thing like it was some prized possession. Not prized, just full of funny memories. The velvet Elvis, a reminder of happier times and that's why each really wants to have it. Awkward couple, trying to have a civil breakup, awkward laughing, talking, recalling purchase of velvet Elvis, who should get it, take it down, hole in wall. Hole in wall! The taking down of the "humorous mask" and unveiling the ugly truth. One of them punched the hole in that wall. Which one? The man? Typical. The woman? Why? The ugly truth. What ugly truth would that be? That one had an affair? Which one? Why? Conflict—darker play.

Monday, April 02, 2001:

Got another hour and a half done on the play. Up to 13 pages, third of way through outline. First fifteen minutes of work was reading over what was already there, readjusting a word here or a piece of punctuation there. Mainly, it gave me time to get back into the heads of my two characters. Was then able to find a smooth transition between where I ended yesterday and the bit of dialog I wanted to include next. Kept going back over the script. Reading from the beginning. Reading it aloud in a whisper (so as not to wake napping son) to find the beats. Raising the tension and then bringing it back down. Exploring the development of the anger and conflict. Roy has become quite a different character than what I have in his character list. Darker, rougher, meaner, less emotional. That's okay, though. The character list is like a safety net. If I get stuck or find that I'm losing my way, I can go back to it and refocus. The structural outline, however, has been extremely helpful. It's always next to me as I work. Makes me feel safe. Let's me know what I'm supposed to be writing and where the conversation needs to go. Prevents me from getting stuck or going off on a tangent.

Thursday, May 03, 2001:

Have reached a difficult spot in the script—the revelation that Roy has been having an emotional affair. For some reason this part is giving me trouble. Probably because explaining Annabel's physical affair is easier, more concrete. What is the definition of an emotional affair? Tried to think about it while washing kitchen floor, but kept going off on tangents in my head. Too many family events coming up and son acting like a typical two-year-old, too many things to get done—brain is distracted. Same thing happened while physically working on it this morning. I should know better than to try to write when my son is up. Too many disturbances from him and the telephone made an already difficult writing session even harder. Unfortunately, son is refusing naps these days—normal two-hour block of writing time is missing and is throwing me off. When all was said and done, I did get about another page completed (out of a probable 4 pages of typing, deleting and retyping). Will try again mid-month when birthdays and Mother's Day is done.

Wednesday, May 23, 2001:

Talked with husband about physical affair vs. emotional affair. Helped to get the male perspective—no big deal to talk to member of opposite sex about intimacies of relationship with spouse. No big deal? Big deal to me, as a woman. I wouldn't want my husband confiding all his hopes/fears about himself and us to another woman. To his best guy friend, as a first stop sounding board before coming to me, okay. But not to another woman. Husband's thoughts helped me get further into Roy's head. Roy no longer seems meaner to me, just different in thinking. Helps me to write for him. Should have remembered you can't write for a character you hate. Each character sees self as good. Husband took son for wagon ride and backyard play, helped me get a solid hour and a half of writing done. Also heard great quote today: "Men cheat because they can get away with it. Women cheat because they aren't getting their needs met." Will ponder on that. Am moving forward.

So, when was the last time your muse paid you a visit: where were you and what were you doing? What thought was planted that triggered your last piece of writing? How long did you think about that idea before you wrote about it? When did you have your best surge of writing over that idea? At what point in the process did you get stuck? How did you resolve your writing problem? How did you keep motivated to finish the project? When will you get your next idea?

Good writing is a process. Good writers love that process. And excellent writers know as much about their process as they do about the technical pieces that go into writing the actual manuscript. De-mystify your writing process by keeping a project journal, and then watch where the journey takes you.

Because it works: Create your own Writing Journal. Choose a notebook or journal book to record the process of any creative writing project you're currently writing. Each time you think about, research, write, or in any other way work on your manuscript, record this in your Writing Journal. Be sure to include the date, start time, end time, and location of where you were when you worked on your piece. Spend the first paragraph describing what you did. Then write another paragraph about how you felt. Did you feel awake or sleepy? Did the time fly because you felt passionate or did time drag because you forced yourself to get the work done? Did you try something new (new pen color, new writing location, different writing time) and if so how did that compare to your normal routine? Keep this journal for the length of your writing project. When you begin a new writing project, start a new section in your Writing Journal devoted to that manuscript. Every three months, review your journal. What patterns can you find that highlight how and when you work best? ❀

Article by Judy Adourian

17

I Can't Write Because . . .

You know the story of Snow White, the seven dwarfs, the wicked witch, the poisoned apple, and Prince Charming. But what happened after "happily ever after?"

Well, Snow White was happy—for a while. But long after the honeymoon was over and Snow White had produced the required number of royal heirs, she became bored. To fill the time, Snow White began to write. Her early efforts were confession stories published in *The Royal Enquirer*. Then she went on to dramatic nonfiction telling the true stories of the princesses in the neighboring kingdoms—Cinderella, Rapunzel, Sleeping Beauty, the Princess who slept on the pea. Snow White wrote under the name of Snow Write to retain some degree of anonymity.

One day when Snow Write was returning from a book signing party at On the Border Book Shop, she passed the woods where the Seven Dwarfs lived and decided to stop in. The little cottage hadn't changed since she'd left, but Snow didn't hear any of the music, dancing, or happy singing that had occupied so much of the dwarfs' days when she lived with them. The seven little men sat solemnly around the kitchen table. Doc sat behind an antique typewriter. The other six each had a pen and a notebook. But nobody was doing anything. Sadness pervaded the cottage.

"Yoo hoo!" Snow Write trilled.

"Hey guys, it's Snow," said Doc. The seven dwarfs rushed to Snow and hugged her around her knees.

"What's the matter?" Snow asked as she kissed each on the top of his little bald head. "You guys look so down."

"We want to be writers like you," Bashful said softly.

"But we can't write!" Grumpy interrupted.

"What do you mean you can't write?" Snow Write said. "Anybody can write."

"We can't," said Sleepy with a big yawn.

"Why not?" asked Snow. "Bashful, you start. Tell me why you can't write."

"Aw gee." Bashful turned away until Grumpy poked him. "Well," Bashful said, "when I was in the third grade in Forest School, I wrote a story about the time my puppy ran away. Everybody in the class laughed at it. I haven't been able to write since."

"That's too bad," said Snow, "but you haven't been in the third grade for decades. It's time to put that old hurt behind you and move on. What about you, Doc?"

"I know I should be able to put a sheet of paper into this typewriter and come out with a complete story, but for some reason it never works."

"That's the funniest thing I've ever heard." Snow laughed. "Nobody writes that way. Writing is a process that takes time. You have to think and plan, write and rewrite, revise and edit."

"Nobody ever told us that," Doc said.

"I have an idea for a story," said Sneezy, grabbing for his handkerchief, "but I can't think of the right opening line."

"Then start with the second line or the third line or the last line. It doesn't matter where you start," said Snow. "Just start. The first line will come to you sooner or later. Write it when it comes."

Dopey started making frantic hand signals. "What's his problem?" Snow asked.

"Dopey says he can't write because he can't spell very well and he doesn't remember the difference between a comma and a semicolon," Doc interpreted. Dopey nodded in agreement.

"There's a lot more to writing than spelling and punctuation," Snow said. "I can help you correct those things. If you have a good story to tell, don't let the mechanics of writing stop you."

The dwarfs relaxed and smiled again. Then a loud thud echoed through the cottage as Sleepy's head hit the table. He woke up quickly, shook his head, and looked around.

"What's your writing problem, Sleepy?" Snow Write asked.

"I've been sitting here all day waiting for inspiration," Sleepy yawned, "but I keep falling asleep. Z-Z-Z-Z."

"You can't *wait* until you're inspired to write," Snow instructed. "You have to play with an idea, a word, or a character. You have to ask 'what if . . .' and experiment with several possible plots. Writing is work, but it's fun, too."

"Not for me," muttered Grumpy. "I hate to write. I only write when I have to. I work better under pressure."

Snow Write scowled right back at him. "No, you don't, silly. You work better when you concentrate. You concentrate when you're under pressure because you're finally forced to. If you allowed enough time to write and concentrated as much at the beginning of the time period as you do when you're down to the deadline, you'd be amazed at what you could write."

"Hummpf," said Grumpy.

"Don't 'hummpf,'" Snow teased. "Just try it; you'll see." She turned to Happy. "What about you? I've never seen *you* sad before."

"I like to write," Happy said, "but I've got writer's block."

"I bet you don't," said Snow Write.

"Yes, I do," said Happy.

"I'll prove you don't. Write, 'Once upon a time there were Seven Dwarfs who . . .'"
Happy wrote quickly. "What did they do?" he asked.

"You tell me," Snow answered.

"They worked in a diamond mine!" shouted Doc.

"A beautiful girl came and lived with them," Bashful added, turning bright red.

"An ugly witch came and tried to poison the girl," continued Sleepy now wide
awake.

"What's Dopey saying?" Snow laughed at the antics of the smallest dwarf.

"He says, 'They kicked the witch into the well and she's never been seen since.'"
Snow Write clapped her hands in delight. "Now you've got the idea. There's no
such thing as writer's block; it's idea block. We just did three things you can do when
you get stuck: brainstorm, write a line and everybody add to it, and start with a familiar
story and change it. You guys even have a built-in writers' group."

"Wow," said Doc, "I just had a great idea. Let's write a book called *Diamond Mining
for Fun and Especially for Profit.*"

"No," argued Grumpy, "let's write an adventure book about getting lost in the mine."

"No, no!" Happy yelled over the others. "Let's write about the time M. Mouse
came from Hollywood to make a movie about us."

"Wait a minute!" Snow Write called for time out. "Each of you should write about
what excites you. You each have different interests. Dopey might like to try poetry,
and Bashful might want to write children's books. There are plenty of choices for
everybody."

Snow Write headed for the door. "I think you guys are on your way. I'll come back
next week to see how you're doing."

"Great," said Doc, "but there's just one more thing."

"What's that?"

"We need some advice about computers?"

"They certainly are great," said Snow Write, "but you don't need one yet. That's
the neatest thing about writing: you can write anytime anywhere as long as you have a
paper and a pencil. But if you do decide to get a computer," she added as she waved
good-bye from the path, "you better stay away from Apples."

Because it works: Think about all the reasons you feel you can't write. Apply Snow
Write's solutions to your reasons for not writing. And then—Write on! ❋

18

Writer's Block Is Not a Writing Problem

Writing isn't hard. Anyone can put words on paper. The hard part about writing is deciding *what* words to put on paper. Unfortunately, the words don't always come as quickly and as smoothly as you'd like. So there you sit, staring glassy-eyed at that glassy screen which is staring back at you. (As much as you'd like to, this is not the time to start playing Free Cell, Spider Solitaire, Pinball, or to catch up on your e-mail correspondence.) Or maybe you're stuck in front of your typewriter, knee-deep in crumpled paper. A blank sheet of paper glares back at you, daring you to try again. But nothing's happening. You have the dreaded **WRITER'S BLOCK.**

In *Writing to Learn* William Zinsser says, "Writing is thinking on paper. Anyone who thinks clearly should be able to write clearly—about any subject at all." This is a major clue to the cause of writer's block. Writer's block is not a writing problem; it's a thinking problem. When you're not thinking correctly, your ability to write becomes blocked.

From my own experience I've determined that there are two kinds of writer's block—major (or long-term) and minor (or short-term). Major writer's block occurs when you can't write a thing—not a paragraph, not a sentence, not word. You can't even put one letter on a piece of paper. Major writer's block develops because other things in your life are in such a state of pain, confusion, or chaos that doing the thinking that writing requires is physically impossible.

My long-term writer's block lasted for about twelve years. I was lucky if I could sign my name to a check, never mind write a weekly grocery list. But I was going through a period of depression. I understand now that it was impossible to be creative or expressive when my whole life was in a pit. At the time it was one more in a long line of frustrations.

Hopefully most writers suffer from the more common short-term writer's block. This occurs because a particular piece of writing just isn't working—you can't come up with that reader-grabbing opening line, you're suffering from mid-novel slump, or the wonderful last line you based the entire poem on no longer fits.

So what do you do about writer's block, short-term or long-term?

When you come to a block, imagine it's because you've just come to a railroad crossing sign that says:

STOP! WAIT! THINK!

It sounds pretty obvious to say, "If you can't write, stop." But that may be just the advice you need. Rather than banging your head against a stone wall when the words aren't coming, it is time to stop and wait. But the waiting time doesn't have to be nonproductive. This is the time to ask yourself some questions.

For major writer's block you will have to think about your life and where you are in it. Ask yourself questions about what you want and what is preventing you from getting it. If you can write at all, this is an excellent time for intensive journal writing. A few weeks or months with your journal may be the impetus you need to break through the block and get your writing life moving. You may require professional help to blast through more difficult problems. The time and money that I invested in professional help was definitely worth the effort.

Short-term writer's block is annoying and frustrating at best. At its worst, it can bring your writing life to a screeching halt. When this happens, it is again time to stop, wait, and think. Minor writer's block can be overcome in one of two ways. The first is to work through the block. The second absolute opposite technique—is to ignore it. Put the problem out of your mind and let your subconscious do the work.

If you decide to work through the block, stop writing and, again, start asking yourself very direct questions about your piece, such as:

Will this piece work better from a different point of view?

Will this piece work better in a different tense or in a different person?

Will the story move again if I add a new element or character? If I remove an element or character?

Is a character acting against his basic nature?

Will a reader-grabbing opening line evolve if I write the middle or the end of my story?

Will the last line of my poem make a perfect opening line? Or be the impetus for a whole new poem?

Just asking questions like these, may be all you need to break through the block. If not, it's time to consult with an objective second party. Call in a trusted writer friend to read your piece. Or share it with your writing group. It's amazing how quickly another knowledgeable writer can pinpoint the weakness or flaw that has you blocked. If the two of you don't find the problem quickly, it's time for discussion and brainstorming. Even if you can't solve the problem on the spot, you'll come away with the benefit of someone else's ideas to think about.

A second Work-Through-It tactic is to stop working on the section that has you blocked and move on to another scene. As you progress in the work, the solution to the problem area will often become apparent, either because the later developments will make clear the resolution or because your subconscious will work on resolving the problem while your conscious brain writes the new scene.

This brings us to the Ignore-It method. Again: stop writing. Put your problem piece away for a time (at least twenty-four hours) and do other things. Take a walk. Listen to music. Work in the garden. Wash the dishes. Do anything that will engage your conscious brain and give your subconscious a chance to solve your thinking problem. You may either experience a moment of sudden enlightenment while you're gardening or in the shower, or the solution may become very obvious the next time you attack your problem piece.

Another Ignore-It technique: program your subconscious to work on the problem while you're asleep. Read the piece over and ask yourself questions about it at bedtime. The answers may come to you just as you're drifting off, waking up, or even in a dream. Be sure to keep paper and pencil next to your bed so you can jot down the answer the minute it occurs to you. Don't wait until morning and expect to remember what came to you in the middle of the night.

No matter how long your writer's block has lasted, it will not become a terminal disease if you diagnose it for what it is—a thinking problem. Then apply both conscious and subconscious thinking exercises that will help you over, under, around, or to blast through the block. Then write on!

Because it works: The next time you get blocked, analyze why you are blocked. Are you experiencing major or minor writer's block? If it's minor, stop writing! Try any or all of the ways listed above to break through the block. ❊

19

Why Can't I Finish This Story?

We all have them—short stories, novellas, and even novels partly written, half-written, almost finished, stories that are finished but just aren't right, and we can't figure out why. They sit in desk drawers, in closets, and in boxes under the bed. They are our ill or ailing fiction—the stories that we won't give up on but for some reason can't finish.

Remember the excitement when you first thought of the idea for the story? Maybe you saw an eccentric character and started writing about her. Or you heard about a strange situation and knew you could turn it into a wonderful story.

You started the story with great eagerness and anticipation. But somewhere into it, the steam ran out, the energy fizzled. And now your wonderful story sits with so many other unfinished works. And you wonder what happened.

There are several reasons why we don't finish the stories we start. They fall into the general categories:

1. Motivation
2. Elemental Problems
3. Structural Problems
4. Fear.

The first question to ask yourself is, "Do you still like the basic idea of your story?"

If the answer is NO, then it's probably time to forget that story. Chalk what you've done up to experience and move on.

If your answer is YES, you have to find out why you haven't or can't finish it.

The first reason may be a simple lack of motivation. Maybe writing just isn't high on your list of priorities right now. Maybe the rest of your life has gotten in the way of your writing life. It does happen. As Liz Aleshire says, "We all have time to write, but the time isn't always right."

At those times you just have to go with the flow, realize that you are in a writing hiatus, and know that it will eventually end.

But let's say you are writing regularly. This story, however, is a thorn in your side, a story that you want to finish.

Motivation

The first motivation solution may be as easy as having a deadline—formal or informal. Would you be motivated to finish this story if an editor promised to publish it and pay you $5,000 as soon as it was done?

I bet you could whip up some motivation. I sure could.

Contest deadlines are another good motivator. (Maybe not quite as good as a promise of publication and payment, but motivation nonetheless.) So is belonging to a writing group. You have to write one scene by the next meeting. You don't have to finish the whole thing, just write one more scene to read to the group the next time it meets. Without my group I know I never would have finished my novella—no group; no motivation; no novella. It's that easy.

Elemental Problems

Okay. You've got the deadline, but you still can't finish the story. Let's look at the possible Elemental Problems. Now's the time to put on your analytical glasses and take an objective look at your story. The first three questions to ask yourself are:

1. Am I writing in the best person? Would my third person story work better in the first person? Or vice versa?
2. Am I writing in the best tense? Should my past tense story be written in the present tense? Or vice versa?
3. Am I writing from the best point of view? Does my point of view character know the most about the story? What will changing the p.o.v. character do to my story? Would *Gone with the Wind* be a different story if it had been written from Rhett Butler's p.o.v.? No doubt about it! Better? Who knows? Try it with your story. See what happens.

Now's the time to experiment. Just take one scene and rewrite it making just one of these changes. Does it feel better? Is it easier to write? If the answer is YES, you're on your way. If the answer is NO, try changing each of these three basic elements and see what happens.

Structural Problems

Problem #1: **Where do I start?**

"The person, tense, and p.o.v. seem fine. I don't think those are the problems," you say.

"Okay, tell me about what you've written so far."

"I've written seventeen pages describing my main character 47-year-old Molly, how she looks, where she works, and everything that happened to her since the trauma of wetting her pants on the first day of kindergarten and I haven't even gotten to the part where she gets a letter on the morning of her marriage to Ernesto (the Brazilian jai alai player) from Casper (her lover and the father of her illegitimate triplets) whom she never stopped loving even though he disappeared in 1972 . . ."

"Hold it! Hold it!" I yell. "If you've written seventeen pages and haven't gotten to (or even hinted at) the conflict, maybe you've started in the wrong place. Try starting your story on her wedding day an hour before the wedding when Molly's sister, Polly, brings her the letter that says Casper has always loved her and is waiting for her behind the gazebo."

Get the idea?

Problem #2: **Where am I going?**

There are as many ways to write a story as there are story writers. But writers can be dumped into two general categories: those who just sit and write to see what happens to their characters, and those who plan out their story before they write. This, obviously, really is a spectrum with every degree of story planner in between.

If you are of the "just write" variety and it works for you, great! Keep it up. But when your story comes to a grinding halt, you may need to sit back and figure out what happened. Ask yourself where am I going and how will I know when I get there? Where have I gotten off the track? Am I digressing?

Even if you are a planner, it may be time to rethink the plan. No plan is carved in stone; it is only a guideline.

Problem #3: **How do I get there?**

The middle of the story is the hardest part for me. But again it's a scene-by-scene process. Knowing the purpose of each scene is the only way to keep on the track. Also keep in mind that the middle is the "muddle"—one obstacle after another that prevents your main character from getting what he or she wants or needs. Making sure that each obstacle is more serious than the previous one will increase the tension and keep the reader in suspense.

Problem #4: **How do I know when I've arrived?**

Ending a story can be just as hard as starting one—especially if you're off the track. This is a matter of going back and finding where you dug yourself into a hole and rewriting out of it.

Sometimes in our eagerness to finish we rush the ending. Or resort to a *deus ex machina* or let-the-reader-figure-it-out-for-himself ending because we don't want to deal with the story anymore. Other times we drag the ending out too long. Thinking about where to stop can help you complete an unfinished story.

Fear

Why would you be afraid to finish a story? For two reasons. The first is that once you finish a story you have to answer the question "Now what am I going to do with it?" The process of submitting and the possibility of rejection can be so daunting that it's easier not to finish the story.

The solution to this one is just to bite the bullet and do it. You have to get over the submission hump at some point. The sooner you do it the better. Rejection is just part of the job. But if you don't submit, you certainly won't ever get published. So again—just do it.

The other side of the coin is the fear of success. Why would anybody be afraid of success? Because if this story (or novel) is wonderful, you're telling yourself, I'll be on the spot. Everybody knows it's harder to write the second novel. And what if an editor wants my story? I don't know anything about contracts or rights or copyright laws. And what happens if my book becomes a best seller? How can I leave the family to do a fifty-city talk show/book signing tour?

We should all have these problems! If you do have to deal with them, take them one at a time, read books and articles, talk to folks who have been published. Find out what the successful writer did.

But first you have to finish that story, novella, novel, or play. So dig it out, dust it off, and analyze why you can't finish it. Then sit down and **write.**

And here's one more thing to think about. In *The Complete Guide to Fiction Writing* by Barnaby Conrad and the staff of the Santa Barbara Writers' Conference, Erica Jong states that for years she never finished anything. She says, "Because, of course, when you finish something, you can be judged."

Those are the problems and the solutions as I see them. There may be other problems and/or other solutions. Dig out your unfinished stories, try some of these suggestions, and then finish them!

Because it works: Take a story you haven't finished out of your drawer. Using the suggestions listed above, figure out why you haven't been able to finish your story. Use as many methods as possible and *finish that story*! ❄

20

The Six P's for a Successful Writing Career

So you want to be a successful writer. So do I. Even though I edit and publish *NEWN* magazine, I'm still a writer struggling to get my work published, just as you are. Sitting on both sides of the desk, so to speak, gives me two views of the writing life. My third vantage point, that of a teacher, produces a strange three-sided desk, but gives me a chance to meet people from all walks of life, some who write as a hobby, others who want to be able to give up their day jobs to become full-time writers.

Whatever your goals and reasons for writing, you are probably looking for tips on how to become a more successful writer. Here are my six P's for a successful writing career:

Prepare: First and foremost, you need to thoroughly understand whatever types of writing you want to do. Whether it's poetry, fiction, nonfiction, or novels, you need a complete understanding of each. Whether it's sci-fi, haiku, tech writing, or plays, you need to read books and articles, take classes, go to workshops to learn what the successful writers in those fields have to say. You need to understand structure and point of view and dialogue and rhythm and rhyme and reason and where to begin and how to bolster a sagging middle and how and when to end.

Second, you need to know your **p.u.g.s.** No, p.u.g.s. doesn't stand for those little dogs with pushed in faces, not in this case. P.u.g.s. stands for *punctuation, usage, grammar,* and *spelling*. Or it could be **g.u.p.s.** But however you spell it, you'd better understand how to punctuate dialogue, when to use *its* and when to use *it's*, how to make clear pronoun references, and whether it's "i" before or after "e." If the old feeling that these things don't matter, that the editor "will fix it up for me" ever *was* true, it isn't any longer. Your manuscript should be as technically perfect as possible.

If I, as a magazine editor, am trying to decide which of two equally good stories to publish and one is riddled with p.u.g.s. errors and the other is error-free, which do you think I'll choose?

Another preparation **P** is: know your **submission p's and q's.** This means always putting your name, address, phone number, e-mail address, and the approximate word count on the first page of the manuscript. It means knowing how to write a cover letter and a query letter. It means always include a SASE. It also means not writing to the editor after your manuscript has been returned to tell her why she should have published it. Many editors hold grudges; the rest of us just have long memories.

The last part of preparation is: **know your markets.** Just reading about a magazine in a marketing column may not give you the entire picture. Because many publications you may be considering are not available in even the largest bookstores, you need to invest some time and a few dollars in sending for sample copies and guidelines. (Many guidelines are available online.) This is the only way to make sure that your work is right for the publication and that the publication is the type and quality you want your work to appear in.

Practice: Now that you know how to write (what you write is up to you), becoming successful becomes a numbers game.

If you wanted to become a concert pianist, my advice would be practice, practice, practice. If you wanted to become a professional golfer, my advice would be practice, practice, practice. If you want to become a gold medal ice skater, my advice would be practice, practice, practice. If you want to be a successful writer, my advice is . . . I think you get the picture.

The more you write, the better you become. It's that simple. And the better writer you are, the better chance you'll get published.

The other part of the numbers game is that the more *kinds* of things you write, the better the chances you'll get published. You may be very happy writing only haiku or short stories or even novels, and you may be great at it. But each market is limited. The more markets you are able and willing to write for, the greater your chances of getting published.

Pursue Opportunities: Now that you're all prepared and practiced, the next step is to pursue any opportunity that comes along. After writing seven proposals for nonfiction books for children (**Perseverance!**), Liz Aleshire was asked by the publisher she had been querying if she'd like to write a book on bugs. Did she *want* to write a book on bugs? No, she wanted to write on the seven other topics she'd suggested. Did she want to get a book published? Of course, she did. Did she write the book on bugs? Of course, she did. *Voilà,* her first published book!

I have done editing for an investment company, I've edited a video script, I've answered ads for writers in local freebie publications, and I've written feature articles for the local newspaper to help the editor out of a jam. None of these endeavors has pulled me away from my main loves (editing *NEWN* and writing fiction), but all were great opportunities to try new areas of writing, all produced a little income to help support my main loves and all added immensely to my experience.

Another word about opportunities—as harsh as this may sound, nobody in the writing world cares whether you or I make it. Nobody's going to call us on the phone and say, "I hear you're a writer. Please send me a story." If you want the world to know that you're a writer, you have to tell them. In other words, you have to create opportunities. You have to tell people that you are a writer.

My friend Judy Nordstrom was working as a guide at Orchard House (the home of Louisa May Alcott in Concord, Massachusetts) and gave a tour to two women. Judy's natural enthusiasm led one of the women to ask if this was her only job. "No," Judy said, "I'm a writer." The woman happened to be a publisher of children's books and was looking for someone to write the history of Concord and Lexington for children. *Voilà*, Judy's first book was published.

I wanted to teach creative writing in our local adult education program, but someone was already teaching it. So I asked myself: "What *doesn't* this program offer?"

What it didn't offer was a basic composition course. So that's what I proposed. Since I had proposed the course in October but didn't hear back from the program director immediately, (See **Patience**), I decided he wasn't interested. He finally called me the next June to say he *was* interested in my proposal. A few years later when I realized the program no longer offered creative writing; I proposed a short story class, which was accepted. What opportunities can you create for yourself?

Perseverance: Okay, you're prepared and practiced and pursuing opportunities, so the next part is easy. Just keep doing it again and again and again and again. Submit, submit, submit, submit. You've heard all the stories of the manuscripts that were turned down twenty-two times but were picked-up on the twenty-third try. What if those writers had stopped at number twenty-two? What if you stop after three tries? Or seventeen? Or fifty? (Jack Canfield's original *Chicken Soup for the Soul* was rejected 144 times!) Those writers persevered. They believed in their work. They didn't quit. They did get published. You can, too.

Patience is probably the hardest **P**. If perseverance is *submit, submit, submit, submit*, patience is *wait, wait, wait, wait*. Unfortunately, things don't often happen in our time frame; they happen in the time frame of the Writing Gods and Goddesses—and there is nothing we can do about it.

Jim (a member of my writing group) waited sixteen months for a decision from an editor on one of his stories. Yes, he did write a polite note inquiring as to the status of his story after about eight months and received a polite "it's still under consideration" which gave him the hope to wait some more. Unfortunately, that hope was dashed when the story was finally returned (after a total of **sixteen** months) and not published. Sorry, not all these stories have happy endings. But Jim has submitted that story elsewhere. And he's waiting again.

What else did Jim and our group learn from his experience? We learned that we won't be in a hurry to submit our work to that publication!

Promote yourself and your writing. You've practiced the first five **P**'s and just received word that your work has been accepted for publication. Now what do you do?

Let the world know!

After my short story won first place in a contest, Janice (another member of my writing group), said: "Send a press release to the newspaper." I procrastinated (another **P** for some of us writers). Janice pushed (that's what's so great about being in a group) until I did it. That release led to an interview and a longer newspaper article about me. And that led to the editor of the paper calling and asking me to write several feature articles when he was in a jam. If I hadn't sent the press release . . . ?

Those are my six **P**'s to becoming a successful writer. Try them and hopefully they'll lead you to the other two P's—the dream of all writers—to be **published** and **paid**!

Because it works: If your writing career isn't where you'd like it to be, think about these **6 P's.** Are any missing from your writing process? Are you spending too much time preparing and never getting to the writing? Are you just procrastinating because you fear rejections? ✱

21

Exciting Writing

I am writing an article. It is about how to make your writing more exciting. It should be an exciting article. So far it isn't exciting. It is boring. I am bored. People who read it will be bored. Z-Z-Z-Z-Z.

Sorry, I just nodded off for a moment there. Almost clunked my forehead on the monitor. See how dangerous boring prose can be?

Let's be clear what I mean by exciting writing. I'm not talking about what to do to make your entire story, poem, or personal essay exciting—that's a topic for another article. I'm talking about making each and every sentence active and alive. How do we do that? Through a number of techniques. But before we discuss those techniques, read the following paragraph:

The Oak City high school basketball team was playing the Central City high school team in the final game of the Regional championship. They had not won a championship in eighteen years. It was overtime. The score was Oak City 91, Central City 92. Billy Mahoney had fouled Johnnie, so Johnnie had this one last chance to win the game. If he made this free throw, he would score two points and Oak City would be the champions. If he missed, he would be the laughingstock of the school and miss his chance to win a basketball scholarship which was the only way he could afford to go to college. Johnnie threw the ball. He missed the basket by one inch. The game was over, so was his life.

Pretty dull, huh? So how do we make our writing exciting?

1. **Use action verbs.** This is probably the most important technique. Recently one of my students showed me a paper her daughter had brought home from her fourth grade class. A tombstone-shaped drawing was titled **dead verbs** with the words *is, are, was, were, has, have, had, and "ing" words* written on the tombstone. We should all draw a tombstone, add these verbs, and hang the picture where we can see it every time we write. These are **telling** verbs (verbs of being), not **showing** verbs.

Go through your latest story and circle every time you used a **dead** verb, then find an **action verb** to replace it.

The most glaring use of these dead verbs is at the beginning of a sentence—especially the opening sentence of your story.

It was the summer that he had turned eight that Daddy had left.

This sentence has a number of problems, so let's just rewrite it:

The summer Harry turned eight Daddy left.

Show us the **action**! But even when you use an action verb, make sure it's the **best** action verb. Instead of writing, *"He walked down the street"* how about a more specific verb—"He sauntered or wandered or trotted or staggered or sashayed or hopped, skipped or jumped down the street." All of these verbs mean "he propelled himself," but each one has a different connotation that adds color and life to the sentence.

Warning! Just make sure the verb you choose is the best word for the image you want portray.

2. **Use a variety of sentence structures**. Certainly writing all simple sentences is boring! But take a look at your writing. Do you overuse compound sentences? Do you frequently start with an introductory clause? Do you often repeat other structure patterns?

Exciting writing contains a variety of sentence structures, including incomplete sentences and sentence fragments, especially in dialogue and internal dialogue.

Warning! Make sure that the two clauses in a compound sentence are related.

We enjoyed a picnic in the park, and I like to ride my bike. (Clauses are **not** related.)

We enjoyed a picnic in the park, and we hope to have another one soon. (Clauses are related.)

I like to ride my bike, and I enjoy roller skating. (Clauses are related.)

Warning: Make sure that the dependant clause and the independent clause in a complex sentence are in the correct order.

We ran for cover as it began to rain. (Wrong order: effect/cause)

As the rain began, we ran for cover. (Correct order: cause/effect)

3. **Punctuate for drama.** How you punctuate a sentence can mean the difference between an ordinary sentence and an exciting one.

"All we do is argue amongst ourselves, and I'm getting sick of it." (We don't usually speak in compound sentences when we are extremely emotional.)

"All we do is argue. I'm getting sick of it!" Use exclamation points sparingly; this one is justified.

"Let me inform you in case you haven't noticed, I've grown-up and those days are over." (Sentence is again too long and is confusing.)

"Let me inform you in case you haven't noticed, I've grown-up. Those days are over."

Or does the writer mean:

"Let me inform you. In case you haven't noticed, I've grown-up. Those days are over."

The more emotional a character becomes the less articulate s/he becomes. Mary isn't going to be speaking in grammatically correct compound/complex sentences when she learns that her husband Carl has just been killed in a car crash. Henry isn't going to render a monologue when he learns that the promotion he expected went to Trent who is twenty-five years younger than he.

4. **Use clear pronoun references.** The writing life would be so much easier without those pesky pronouns, but we must deal with them. A pronoun is a substitute for a noun and, hence, it must refer to the correct noun (antecedent). In the middle of our basketball example, we have a lot of **he.** We need to make it clear which boy we are referring to in each case.

5. **Remember T.E.D.—Tension, Emotion, Drama.** Your story should not be just a series of events. It needs emotion. Emotion leads to tension. Tension leads to drama. Drama adds excitement to your writing. So organize your material for maximum drama. Look at this example:

   Finding the office on the fifth floor, she paused, ran a practiced hand through her hair and walked confidently into the office. "Mr. Hubbard? I'm Laura Allen. I'm here about the executive assistant position." A glance at the wall clock let her know she was on time, just.

   Consider rearranging the sentences into not only a more natural order but also a more dramatic order.

   Finding the office on the fifth floor, Laura paused and ran a practiced hand through her hair. A glance at the wall clock let her know she was on time—just. She walked confidently into the office. "Mr. Hubbard? I'm Laura Allen. I'm here about the executive assistant position."

6. **Details, details, details.** Exciting writing is full of details and sensations. Details make images concrete. Sensory details make the reader feel what the character feels.

   Sam saw the man drive away in a late model station wagon.
   Sam saw the suspect peel out of the parking garage in a 1999 red Explorer.
   Cindy Lou put polish on her toenails.
   Cindy Lou put Dragon Lady Red polish on her toenails.

7. **Concentrate on people**, not on abstract ideas.

   It was a sleepy little town where nothing ever happened. Many teenagers left as soon as they could.

   Watertown is the pits, Marshall thought. I'm out of here as soon as I turn eighteen.

   Two weeks to go, Marshall thought, and I'll be eighteen and out of this burg. Watertown sucks. I'm off to see the world.

8. **Try changing person or tense.** Would your piece be more exciting in the first person rather than the third, or in the present tense rather than the past tense? Experiment to see which works best.

9. **Cut out clichés and make sure similes and metaphors are appropriate**.
    The ball missed the basket by an inch. (Cliché.)
    Officer Jones ran through the streets of New York City like a panther across the Serengeti Plains. (Find a simile having to do with the city.)

10. **Show; don't tell**. All of this boils down to that wonderful phrase that we hear constantly—show; don't tell.

11. **My last suggestion to make your writing exciting is to be excited about your writing**. We all get bogged down in the middle (especially on a long project) and often revert to telling just to finish the story. We need to sustain or reignite our initial enthusiasm to make the ending as exciting as the beginning.

Here's how I would use the Rules for Exciting Writing to make the basketball scene more exciting:

Thud. Thud. Thud. The cheers of the crowd all but drown out the hollow sound of the basketball as I bounce it at the free throw line. But I can feel the thud reverberating in my head—and in the pit of my stomach.

Thud. Thud. Thud. I glance at the score board HOME 91—VISITORS 92. Five seconds to go in overtime. Central City has us by one lousy point. Thanks to Jason Turner fouling me, it's all up to me.

This is it. My last chance. The "make it or break it" basket. If I make the shot, we win the championship—the first for Oak City High in eighteen years. If I miss—well, my college scholarship and my whole basketball career are literally on the foul line with me. But I can't allow myself to think about that.

"Concentrate," I tell myself, "just concentrate."

Thud. Thud. Thud.

The ball slips through my hands as I bounce it. Sweat stings my eyes. I swipe my hand across my forehead. The chant of the crowd grows louder and louder:

Zack! Zack! Zack!

Brings us

Back! Back! Back!

The screaming, the chanting, the pounding in my head close in on me.

The piercing blast of an air horn startles me, and the ball leaves my hand of its own volition. It arches high, descends gracefully right over the basket, then drops landing on the rim.

The screams of the crowd ricochet from wall to wall.

The ball circles the rim. Once. Twice. Then falls—to the floor.

The buzzer grates into my brain severing me from my future. The Central City bleachers explode into cheers. I fall to my knees and pound the floor.

Thud. Thud. Thud.

Note: A staff member told me that a free throw is for one point and one basket would just tie the game. Also a great basketball player would probably not lose his scholarship by losing one game, even a championship game. I appreciate these corrections, but I have to let my original situation stand because it's too late to change it (and I do like the drama and tension that the situation creates).

Because it works: Take a look at a piece you've written. Get rid of the dead verbs, the clichés, and the telling. Use action verbs, scenes that show, and dramatic punctuation. See how much more exciting your writing is! ✱

22

The Write Place

My office is a mess. I mean a real mess. Piles of papers cover the table that is my desk. More piles are on the floor. Everywhere I look there are stacks of books and magazines that I mean to read and then file. Not to mention the clippings that I've cut out of magazines and newspapers that I plan to read—someday. And the piles of my own "works-in-progress."

As soon as this issue of *NEWN* is out of my hands, as soon as I'm done teaching for the semester, I'm going to clean my office. I'm going to file and organize, neaten and tidy it for good. Well, at least until it gets messed up again.

Does that sound like a lot of work? I'm sure it will be. But it will also be a labor of love because I have an office—a place of my own. When my daughter Judy moved out, she gave me one of the greatest birthday gifts ever—the time and the work to turn her old bedroom into my office. We cleaned everything out of her old bedroom, painted the walls, bought a new rug and valances and bought and constructed file drawers and bookcases (with help from our electric screwdriver that was worth its weight in gold). We moved all my books out of the tiny room I had kept stuff in (but couldn't turn around in) and arranged them on their new shelves. Then Judy helped me organize my file drawers so that I can actually find things that I'm looking for—most of the time.

Why do I tell you all this? Because all writers need a place of their own. If you can beg, borrow, or negotiate an entire room of your own, that's great. But even if you can't, you need an area, a nook, a cranny, a closet, a corner of the dining room where you can keep all your writing stuff and have everything close at hand so that when you can make the time to write, you don't have to worry about where you're going to do it.

I know, you're going to tell me you're much more creative in the den with a glass of wine or at the beach or under the pine trees in the backyard. And that may be true—when you're in a creative phase—but eventually you have to apply fingers to typewriter or computer. Eventually you have to deal with the business of writing and organization. Eventually you have to deal with your left brain as well as your right brain and make order out of what can easily become chaos.

Organization doesn't come easily to me; it's still a chore and I'm sure always will be. I still lose and misfile things. And cleaning my office will undoubtedly take longer than whatever amount of time I allow for it. Maybe organization is work for you, too. But it's worth the effort. Why? Picture this:

Weeks ago you sent a story to *Wonderful Stories Magazine*. Today you get a phone call from the editor who says, "We love your story. We want to publish it. We want to pay you $1,000 for your wonderful story."

"Wonderful!" you say.

"There's just one problem," she says, "We want to suggest a couple of changes."

"No problem," you say.

"I want to go over the changes on the phone. Do you have a copy handy?"

"Oh." Now you have a problem. Where did you put your copy?

Maybe this doesn't apply to you; maybe you have the write place and are wonderfully organized. I hear there are people like that. If not, I'd like to suggest a couple of books. The first is *Organizing for the Creative Person* by Lehmkuhl and Lamping (Crown Trade Paperbacks). The second is *A Room of One's Own* by Virginia Wolf. I plan to read it again—soon after I clean my office. It's at the bottom of one of those piles on the floor

Because it works: Arrange for a writing area in your home. Furnish it with whatever you have space for—especially a filing cabinet. If you already have an office, schedule some time to make it neat and tidy. Then keep your writing area organized. ✻

23
Happy New Writing Year

The calendar says the New Year starts on January first. Mother Nature says the New Year begins with the birds and flowers of spring. We each face a new year when we celebrate our birthday.

But for me, another new year starts in September when school reopens. From 1971 when my son entered nursery school to the present day, someone in our family has started a new academic year each fall. When I returned to college in 1983 to complete my Bachelor's degree, the tradition was reinforced. After graduating, I moved to the other side of the desk and began teaching through a local adult education program. So now the Autumn New Year is ingrained in me forever.

The start of a new academic year is a perfect time to take a look at your writing life, where you are now and where you hope to go in the next year. Here are four things to consider:

First, **make a list of everything you've written** in the past year and decide if you're pleased with what you've accomplished. If you aren't, it's time to ask yourself some very basic questions. I firmly believe that some of us are by nature essayists, some are poets, some epic novelists. What we have a natural affinity for, we write most easily. We may have to try many areas of writing before we each find our comfort niche—the writing we were meant to do.

This is not to say that we can't write in more than one area. But if you feel you're banging your head against your monitor, it may be because you're writing the wrong stuff. If you've written twenty-seven pages of your epic novel and you've said it all, maybe you're really a short story writer. If, on the other hand, your short-short story turns out to be seventeen chapters and you're still going, maybe you're really a novelist.

This is the perfect time **to take an adult education class**. You might take a writing class, but you might consider a class in some subject you've always wanted to study (astrology, Greek cooking, or medieval history) that could make a great subject for a novel, story, poem, or article.

Find a writing group through your local library. Or start a writing group. Find several other writers of the same genre and interests, find a time and a place to meet, and you're on your way to creating the kind of support network we all need.

And if you've always wanted to go to or return to college, don't wait any longer. **Do it now!**

Take time. No, **make time to write**. You will never *find* enough time in your busy life to write. If you're serious about developing your writing career, you'll have to *make time.*

Get up half an hour earlier. Stay up half an hour later. Write on your lunch hour. Write on the weekends. Write during the winter and market your work during the summer. Don't worry about what anyone else does. Figure out what works best for you. That's the only thing that matters.

Don't let this one scare you. **Make goals.** Goals are not intended to stress you out. They are meant to keep you on track. Be reasonable and keep in mind your level of writing experience and the amount of time you can devote to writing. Consider goals that include writing, marketing, and developing your craft.

By taking a look at your writing life, understanding what you have a natural affinity for, making time, and making some realistic goals, you can have a very Happy New Year Writing!

Because it works: On whatever date you decide to be your New Year, make a list of everything you wrote during the past year. Then make a list of what you want to accomplish during the up-coming year. Stick to your plan! ❈

SHARING—BECAUSE WRITERS NEED OTHER WRITERS

24

Are YOU Ready To Critique or Be Critiqued?

Sure, you've finished your essay on Uncle Ethan, your poem on pleasure, that short story about Hemingway's Hems, or, those first elegant chapters of your novel: *Not Without Nuisance*. You've evaluated your idea, outlined, first drafted, applied the seat of your pants to the chair, and sweated. You've **re**-written, **re**-drafted, **re**-outlined, quit, returned, quit again, and still came back for more. You're eager to show it to someone. Anyone. Your mother perhaps. Or a spouse, your children, a neighbor, your best friend. You wrote to be read, right? These are the best readers for your finely honed work, right?

Wrong! Or, maybe not. Do they (or you) know how to critique? Most of us wouldn't presume to go past "I like it" or "I don't like it" when viewing art work. We wouldn't presume to cast judgment on a sculpture—or a bold new architectural development. We wouldn't use tone-deaf ears to fuel a mouth critiquing an opera by a new composer. Not unless we were well educated and experienced in art, sculpture, architecture, or opera, or at least knew the rules that govern a critique of those works.

So why trust a layman with writing you might have slaved over for seven days, seven weeks, seven months, or even seven years? Your first step to getting an effective critique of your writing is to find someone who knows how, or someone you can teach how, to read a piece of writing and critique the writing instead of the style and content.

What's that mean? Imagine you've passionately worked on an essay about the horrors of pet neutering. You pass the piece off to your best friend who gives you a critique on the joys and advantages of pet neutering. That's not what you wanted. What you, the writer, most need to know is: Did I get my point across? Did you like my protagonist and hate my villain? Was it funny? Was it sad? How did you feel at the end of my piece? Imagine finding out just after you've mailed a humorous essay to a magazine editor that your best friend cried when he read it? If you think you're writing humor and your readers are crying, you're doing something wrong. If your readers think the protagonist is a wimp but really love the villain, you're doing something wrong. If your readers don't express a feeling after reading your piece, you're doing something wrong. A critique is not the opening gambit for a highbrow (or lowbrow, for that matter) discussion, no matter how enjoyable the debate may be. The purpose of a critique is to let you know when you've written wrong. To get, or give, an effective critique, both the author and the reader must follow a few rules. Each side has its own set of responsibilities in the process.

The Critiquer's Responsibility:

1. **Critique the writing not the subject matter.** The writer doesn't care if you agree with the story's premise. The writer wants to know if she got her point across. Did she? If she didn't, say so. You don't have to think up twenty ways to change the piece—that's the author's job. And, you don't have to agree with the author's point of view to evaluate effective writing.
2. **Always start a critique with the positive points.** A little praise for the author at the beginning softens the blow of pointing out the weak points.
3. **Be gentle but not too kind.** Tactful but honest. If you don't think the writer communicated the point to you, say so. If you think the characterization is weak but like the story line, say so. If you're wondering what the point of the whole exercise was, say so. That's your job.
4. **Never just say you liked a piece of writing.** Take some time and let the writer know why you liked it. I recommend that critiques be done in writing. With the exception of writing classes or groups, I'd rather my critiquer take the material home, read it, live with it, and give a well-thought-out assessment. Comments made off-the-cuff can be misleading. And, reading a piece of writing to a group is not the same as silent reading. Much more is absorbed in silent reading than when we listen to a piece being read. Take it home, take the time, and do it all in writing.
5. **When reading a book excerpt, remember that you are critiquing only a portion of the entire work.** Assume that prior and later chapters do a lot to explain the action in the current piece and concentrate solely on what's in front of you without being overly concerned about what comes before or after.
6. **Insist that a list of writing questions accompany the manuscript** but don't read them until after you've read the author's work. Answer the writer's questions as honestly, objectively, and as helpfully as you can. Refuse to critique something if the author wants to know "do you like it." Reading tastes vary widely among families and friends. You don't have to like science fiction to critique it adequately. It helps to know the genre you're critiquing, but it isn't required. Clear, concise communication is recognizable on any topic.
7. Most important: **Never critique style.** This is the most difficult part of a critiquer's job—especially if you're also a writer. Whenever you're tempted to say "Well, I would have written it thus and so," STOP! That's your style asserting itself and

your comments will not help the author. Don't tell the author how you would have written it. Tell the author if she wrote effectively even if it isn't the way you would have done it.

The Writer's Responsibility:

1. Try your best not to take a critique personally. You won't find many people willing to do the work of a critique if you're angry or sniffling over the results.
2. Don't cave in! You know your story better than the reader. Learn to cull out the statements that aren't relevant. And learn to support your words with an expert's knowledge of your story. Change something only when there seems to be a consensus among the critiquers that there is an area that needs work. If each critiquer highlights a different "weakness," then everything is probably all right with the piece and nothing should be changed. But, if three critiques all mention a weakness in character development, then it's probably true and you need to go back to writing.
3. Ask specific questions that can't be answered with a *yes* or *no*. If you think about it, you know where your areas of weakness are. Ask how the reader feels about the dialogue. The pacing? What is the dominant impression of the main character? The villain? Do the critiquer's answers match with your intent? If they do, you've written well. If they don't, go back to writing.
4. If the critique focus is on style, get another critique. You'll know the focus is on style if your reader makes comments like: "I would have used the word 'penultimate,'" or "I would make the grandmother jump off the cliff in the fifth chapter!" Pat yourself on the back because you've enthralled a reader and made him think. But what he's thinking about is how he'd write the story not how effectively you wrote it.
5. Always reciprocate. You'll find most often that your best critiquers will be the writing friends you make through classes and conferences. If you trust your reader, be a good reader in return. You scratch in red on my manuscript, and I'll scratch in red on yours.
6. Be patient. The best critiques are done with a silent reading. Yes, it helps to read aloud to a group and get their gut reaction. But an in-depth critique, the kind you're looking for, takes time. Always give the critiquer a copy, while you keep the original, and let her live with it for awhile. You want a well-thought-out answer not something spur of the moment.

It's of equal value to be a reader and a critiquer. You'll be surprised how much you'll learn about your own writing from reading and evaluating someone else's. Feedback is important to your writing development. There'll come a day when you won't need anyone else reading your work to tell you if you've hit the mark. You'll know on your own. Until that time, read and be read by someone who knows how.

Because it works:

1. Find a piece of writing you have never shown anyone, or write a new piece.
2. Edit and revise it up to three times.
3. Read it over.
4. Make a list of questions you'd want a reader to answer. Hint: *Did you like it?* should NOT be on your list?
5. Some examples: (You may come up with different questions)
   a. Did you like my protagonist?
   b. Did you hate my antagonist?
   c. Did I answer my story question? Did my protagonist get what he/she wanted?
   d. Is my dialogue believable?
   e. What emotion did you feel reading this piece?
   f. Was there anything that didn't make sense, anything that you didn't understand?
   g. What does my protagonist want? What's the motivation?
6. Then, have a trusted writer friend or colleague read the piece and answer the questions. How close were the reader's answers to your intentions? The closer your reader's answers match your intentions, the better your writing. ✿

Article by Liz Aleshire

25

Critique Unto Others as You Would Have Them Critique You

One of the reasons writers need other writers is to get objective, constructive criticism on works in progress. But getting good feedback isn't always easy. Here are several things to consider from the standpoint of being both the writer and the critiquer:

You-the-Writer

First, you need to respect the opinion of the critiquers. Don't ask just anyone for an opinion. Even within a writing group, there may be some people whose opinion you value more than others. Be sure you are familiar with the background and experience of the critiquers.

Second, know what you want from the critiquers. When requesting feedback, don't ask, "What do you think?" or "Do you like it?" You-the-Writer need to ask specific questions, such as:

Does my story start at the right point?

Did the opening grab you?

Are my characters believable?

Did I write from the best point of view?

Does my dialogue sound natural? Does it advance the plot?

Is the setting (time, location, and mood) vivid and accurate?

Is the ending satisfying?

Or you might ask, "I'm having trouble with the transition between scene A and scene B. Can you suggest another way of doing it?"

The more information you can give the critiquers regarding how you see the story and what you need from them, the better their critiquing will be.

You-the-Critiquer

Good critiquing can be accomplished only through a complete understanding of all the elements of the genre being critiqued. By having a check list of questions, your critiquing (whether in a group or as an individual) will be objective, stay focused, and not deteriorate into an expression of personal likes and dislikes.

Over and above the specific feedback the writer asks for, a good critiquer should be aware of other problems that can show up especially in the work of beginning writers. You-the-critiquer should watch for:

- Subtle (and not so subtle) shifts in point of view.
- Incorrect facts and details the author missed. (She has blue eyes on page 3 but has brown eyes on page 17 or reference to the "Roman god Zeus" when the Roman god was Jupiter.)
- Any statements that are vague or unclear.
- Unclear dialogue (needs more tags).
- Dialogue with too many tags and too many direct addresses.
- Monologues instead of conversation.
- Too much telling; not enough showing.
- Too much or unnecessary description.
- Are there scenes that should be dramatized rather than narrated? Are there scenes that should be narrated rather than dramatized?
- Are there scenes that do nothing to advance the plot or show characterization?
- Flashbacks that are confusing possibly because of verb tense or transition problems.
- Intrusion of author's bias.
- Does the story flow smoothly? Is it choppy?
- An unsatisfying ending that cheats the reader.

It is very difficult to concentrate while listening to the reading of a long story or novel excerpt, so think about critiquing from written copy. Whether your group brings copies for every member or mails them for members to read in advance, the effort can be worth the extra time and cost because you will get better feedback.

Critiquing should always be done kindly and with the sensitivity of the writer in mind. Start with comments on what you liked about the piece and then move on to how the writer can make the piece better. Always remember how you feel when you're on the receiving end of the critiquing.

I attended a writing conference several years ago. One evening an impromptu critiquing group evolved. I didn't know anyone in the group, so I debated whether or not to read a story. I finally decided I was there to get feedback and so I should participate.

As the critiquing of my story began, some helpful suggestions were offered. But as the session went on, one member of the group said, "You know you could change the ending to . . ." Nobody had said that my ending didn't work, but soon the others chimed in with their suggestions as to how I could change the ending. I knew the critiquing had become personal opinion and each participant was now writing the story the way he wanted it to end. I thanked the group for their advice, made use of the helpful suggestions—and ignored the rest.

Because it works: Read stories you have written as a critiquer instead of as a writer or a reader. Be as kind to yourself as you would be to another writer. But also be firm about what isn't working in each story. Critique the writing; don't beat yourself up because the story isn't perfect. **Writing is rewriting!** ❋

With Liz Aleshire

26

Writers Need Other Writers; Writers Need You

Writers need other writers. No matter the writer's age, gender, genre or expertise, every person who tackles this solitary creative profession, whether for pleasure or profit, needs other like-minded individuals for support, encouragement, and education. That's why I was thrilled to conduct a poetry workshop for 9-14 year olds at Willow Books in Acton, Massachusetts, in April 2001. Six young poets braved the rainy weather to join me for an hour discussion about rhyme, rhythm, meter, and form. I began the workshop with the hope of becoming an inspirational mentor to at least one future poet. I ended up learning more than I taught.

After introducing ourselves, I began the workshop by asking "Why do you write poetry?" Two admitted they write poetry because they had gotten tired of writing short stories. Another two said that poetry helps them express their feelings. The other two simply enjoyed the fun of writing. Sound familiar? I started writing poetry when I was eight to express my feelings (yes, even eight-year-olds feel stress). I continued writing poetry because I found it fun. After a while, I tired of poetry and ventured into short stories, plays and now personal essays. Despite the twenty years that separated my age to theirs, we already had a common bond as writers.

Why do you write?

One of the girls said she writes a poem a day. Her mother concurred saying: "We find her poetry all over the house." A poem a day. Even I, a "professional writer," don't have the self-discipline to write every day. Even though I know that like any other craft practice makes perfect, I still make excuses at least twice a week as to why I can't write that day. It's too rainy. It's too sunny. I'm too busy. I've finally got a moment to myself.

How often do you write?

We talked about syllables, stresses, rhythm, rhyme, similes and metaphors. Ever tried to explain what a metaphor is to a fourteen-year-old? You may think you know what a metaphor is. I thought I knew. But once that teenager starts asking you questions, you'll realize that it's been much too long since you reviewed the basics. How about a contradictory statement as it applies to haikus? Do you know? Could you explain it?

When was the last time you reviewed the basics?

We clustered (or webbed, as it's now called in school) on the word "tree." The next time you think you have writer's block, cluster and brainstorm with the nearest writer, child or adult. Tossing around words and ideas with other people will carve out a multitude of windows and doors in your block. Soon you'll be complaining that you have too many ideas and not enough paper and ink to write them all down. And not once did I hear "Don't take my idea . . ." or "I can't write about that." I for one am highly guilty of keeping my ideas to myself for fear of jinxing my ability to then write about it. "What are you working on?" my own husband will ask as I'm typing on the computer. "A play," I answer, minimizing the screen so he can't sneak a peek.

When was the last time you brainstormed with a group?

I then asked them each to write a four line poem in ABAB form where the last word of each line had to be "leaves," "roots," "bees," and "boots" respectively. Even I joined in the fun. Together, we seven poets jumped from the same starting point and landed in seven distinctly different places. I can't remember the last time I played this kind of poetry game, but from the surprisingly good results I got, I should do it more often.

When was the last time you really challenged yourself or played with words?

Finally, five of us read our pieces aloud to the group. I haven't read my poetry to a group since freshman creative writing? Those of us who read were thanked with excited applause. Our other two more timid members chose not to read their pieces aloud, but were still given the same unconditional applause for their efforts.

When was the last time you supported and encouraged another writer?

Because it works: Find several other writers through your local library or book store and start your own writers' group. Teach the others how to critique by using our suggestions. You'll see very quickly how much writers need other writers.

Article by Judy Adourian

27

When You're Not Ready to Share

After I gave the first assignment to a new class last fall, one student said, "I know what I want to write about, but it wasn't a very happy situation and my husband won't like it."

"Don't read it to your husband," I said.

She looked puzzled. "But what'll I say?" she asked.

In the moment before I answered that question, my mind flashed back to 1965. I had been married for a couple of years and had just enrolled in the Famous Writers Correspondence Course. After completing my first assignment, I was very excited and read it to my husband expecting he would tell me I was well on my way to a Pulitzer Prize. He listened dutifully and then said, "You said the framus on the car was broken. It should have been the widget."

I was crushed and never read another assignment to my husband.

I did complete the correspondence course and made a few unsuccessful attempts at submitting my work. Then I stopped writing for about eleven years. I won't go into all the reasons for this hiatus, but what they added up to was the complete degeneration of my writer's ego.

When I resumed writing in the early 1980's, I started very slowly. I wrote what I liked, what made me happy. I realized that I needed feedback from other writers, so I joined a local writers' group. I went to workshops and talked and listened to many other writers. I decided whose opinion I respected and whose I didn't. I asked for advice from those I respected, but I realized that even that was only an opinion.

Now I have special people I ask to critique my work. If I want to read a story to my husband, I say, "I just wrote the best story I've ever written and I'm going to read it to you."

When I'm done and he points out that I'm still confusing the framus with the widget, I say, "Thanks, I'll change that. You're the expert on the technical stuff, but isn't this the best story I've ever written?"

He's learned to say, "Yes."

So I told my student and the rest of the class, "Tell your husband that your teacher says you are not allowed to read your story to anybody except her." She brightened as I continued, "You are all beginners. If you read your beginning work to friends and family, they will do one of two things. They will tell you it's wonderful or they'll ask what makes you think you can be a writer. Either answer can be devastating."

I explained that Mom, Aunt Tillie, and your best friend are *supposed* to tell you your writing is great. That's their job. But what happens if the rest of the world doesn't agree? There goes your writer's ego.

If you get the other reaction—what makes you think you can be a writer?—you will begin to doubt your talent, your desire, and your dream. There goes your writer's ego.

If you're not ready to share your work with family and friends, tell them your editor says you're not allowed to read it to anybody but her. I'll back you up.

Here's another awkward situation when you might not be ready to share:

At a recent writers' conference I read a portion of a student's story as an example of an excellent beginning. After the conference, the writer told me that another participant told him how much she loved what had been read. "I'd love to read the rest of the story," she said. "Would you send me a copy?"

"What did you say?" I asked the writer.

"I said I would," he answered.

"Why?" I asked.

"Why? Because she asked me to . . . I guess."

I could understand that the writer was flattered, but it also put him in an uncomfortable position. He didn't really want to send his complete story to another writer, but he also didn't know what to say.

"Just because she asked for a copy doesn't mean you have to send her one," I said.

"But what do I say?"

"Try this," I suggested. "Say, 'I'm really pleased you liked my story. Send me a self-addressed, stamped envelope and after it's published I'll send you a tear sheet'."

As I've thought about this incident, I wonder how many of us have been put in that awkward position and didn't know what to say? Or have asked for a copy of a story or a poem we've heard read—not realizing that we've put the writer in an awkward position? I have.

Would we go to a show at an art gallery and say to the artist, "Gee, I really like that painting. Would you send me a copy?"

Would we attend a concert and say to the performer, "That was a great aria you sang. Please send me a tape of it."

So if you're not ready to share but don't know what to say, try the above suggestions.

Because it works: Pass these suggestions on to other writers who may not know what to do if they are asked for a manuscript. ❈

28

With Thanks to Jim, Ann, Donna, Carleen, and Janice—Or Why You Should Join A Writer's Group

I am writing a novella. I call it a novella because it's much too long to be a short story and nowhere near long enough to be a novel. This work is longer than anything I have ever written—14,000 words and counting. As much as I love to write, for me the hard work of writing, the labor of writing, is completing that first draft. I have a drawer full of uncompleted stories that I like to call "works in progress." If I were honest, I'd call them what they really are—stuff I've given up on, usually in the middle of the first draft.

In the last couple of years, however, I've dug out and resurrected some of those stories. I've completed several and even won a contest with a piece I wrote about ten years ago but had never done anything with. So what happened in the last couple of years to kick my writing career into higher gear?

I joined a writing group.

Every other Monday night some combination of the six group members meets at one of our homes. We bring in short pieces that we read and critique on the spot. We bring in copies of longer pieces to take home, read, and critique. We bring in stories that aren't working, discuss the problems, and receive the combined wisdom of the group—solutions and ideas that none of us would come up with on our own.

As I said before, it's easy for me to give up on long pieces. So why hasn't this happened with my novella? Because I committed to writing at least one new scene every two weeks to bring to the group.

At this point it isn't even a matter of wanting my work critiqued. I'll need that when I start revising my first draft. Right now my group provides the structure, the external deadline, the reasons that keep me writing. I have no excuses for quitting. I can't let the group down; they're waiting to hear what happens next. And they're giving me what I need—a pat on the back for writing one more scene.

So there *you* sit. You've just finished a story, a poem, an essay—or maybe even your novel—and you've lost all objectivity. Is it good? Bad? Or maybe you're into a piece of writing and you're stuck. Something's not working, but you're not sure what. Or you've lost your motivation to finish what you've started. What can you do?

You need to find a group of your own.

I once heard an author say that all writers are introverts who only want to sit alone in a room and write. Any **all** statement is dangerous, and I certainly didn't believe that one. But writing is a solitary activity; it doesn't, however, have to be a lonely one. Most writers need to associate with other writers. A writers' group can be an excellent source of stimulation, inspiration, motivation, critiquing, and socializing.

It's time to get back to my novella. It's Monday afternoon at 5:00 p.m.; My Group meets at 7:30. But I will have the first draft of another scene to take with me—because My Group is expecting it. I don't know how long it'll take for me to finish my novella, but I've already written the acknowledgements: With thanks to Jim, Ann, Donna, Carleen, and Janice without whom this work would still be "in progress."

Because it works: Find or create your own writing group at your library, a bookstore, or in the homes of other writers. ❀

Other Genres—
Because You Need to Stretch

29

Laughing All the Way to the Bank

Writing humor is not easy. But, boy, is it needed.

I began researching the subject of humor in my writing library and found that I had the following: one book on how to write for comedians (jokes, gags, and one-liners and writing sitcoms), one anthology of American humor, and one volume of light verse. Nothing on how to add humor to fiction, essays, and poetry. This definitely required a trip to the book store. (Heaven forbid I should do research at the library!) The result of that trip was that I now have three books on how to write for comedians, two humor anthologies, a book of light verse, and a $50 charge on my Visa card.

I then began researching other writing books. I found one chapter on writing humor in *The 30-Minute Writer* by Connie Emerson. Connie mentions six forms of humorous writing.

1. **Light humor:** poking gentle fun at our human natures and probably the most salable form.
2. **Irony:** saying exactly what you don't mean.
3. **Exaggeration:** exaggerating any facet of everyday life, usually a frustrating one.
4. **Satire:** humorously writing about things that aren't usually considered funny.
5. **Parody:** Imitating the style and content of a well-known story, movie plot, or TV show, but using a different subject.
6. **Off-the-Wall:** looking at a subject upside-down, sideways, or from some totally crazy angle.

In the November 1996 issue of the *American Writer Review*, television and comedy writer John Vorhaus gives "Six super tools from the comic toolbox" (which leads me to wonder if six is some kind of magic funny number).

1. **Clash of context:** the forced union of incompatible ideas or persons, such as in *Crocodile Dundee, Northern Exposure, Green Acres,* and *The Beverly Hillbillies.*
2. **The wildly inappropriate response** which, like clash of context, involves the juxtaposition of emotions and attitudes. As an example, Vorhaus suggests scenes from the movie *Cat Ballou* (one of my all-time favorites).
3. **The law of comic opposites,** such as in Oscar and Felix in *The Odd Couple.*
4. **Tension and release** in which every joke creates tension; the punch line releases the tension. The longer you can delay the punch line, the funnier the joke will be. Vorhaus suggests watching the cliff jumping scene from Butch Cassidy and the Sundance Kid.
5. **Telling the truth for comic effect:** Just stating the obvious can be extremely funny. My favorite example is Jay Leno reading real headlines.
6. **Telling a lie for comic effect:** That is reversing the truth of a situation.

One summer at the International Women's Writing Guild Conference I attended a week long workshop titled "Writing Down the Funny Bones: The Women's View of Comedy" led by Anne Walradt from New Jersey. For six days from nine o'clock in the morning until 10:15, twenty-five women sat in a classroom, talked about humor, read humor, and laughed. What a great way to start a day—what a great way to start every day!

One of the points that Anne made during her workshop was that humor connects us to our audience, to our readers. She quoted Victor Borge who said "Laughter is the shortest distance between two people."

Anne pointed out that humor illustrates and "punctuates" points and ideas, thus making it easier for the reader to understand and learn. She said that humor also diffuses tension and conflict, makes bad news more palatable, and increases retention of the message.

Anne emphasized the one common point made in every humor writing source I researched: "Writing effective humor is not easy. The first thing you need is a natural sense of humor, the tendency to look at the world a little off-center. If you cope with the annoyances or pain of life with wryness or laughter, if you find others chuckling over your words, intentionally or inadvertently, humor writing may be for you."

"If your outlook on life tends to be dour, angry, or depressed," she added, "you may have a harder time writing humor."

Here are five techniques that Anne suggested to help us "increase our humor quotient and strengthen our funny bone."

1. **Exaggeration:** typified by the "How hot is it?" joke.
2. **Affectation:** Anne found affectation at a concert. The soloist sang "Old Mother Hubbard" as an aria. The pretentiousness of a nursery rhyme sung as dramatic opera sent tears of laughter rolling down the cheeks of the listeners.
3. **Incongruity:** A gorilla goes into a bar and . . .

4. **Repetition:** Anne said that it's the third time something is said or done that usually makes it funny. But repetition can be tricky to use. Writers of solemn material take note here; do not let the same thing appear three times. You may lose your audience because of unintended humor.
5. **Mechanization:** describing humans as objects, as animals, or as characteristics (Mrs. Fidget or Miss Conception).

One of Anne's and my favorite humorists will always be Erma Bombeck who connected with her readers through humor we can all identify with, like:

"Sometimes I wake my son up in the middle of the night and ask him to smile. Those braces that twinkle in the darkness represent my fur coat, my trip to Monaco, my second car, my college education, my insurance policy . . ."

I recently scanned two books. The first was *Comedy Workbook* by Gene Perret. This should be hilarious, I thought. Well, the examples Perret used (jokes and one-liners) were funny. But his writing about comedy was very serious.

The subject of the second book was how to write great ad copy which I did not expect to be a humorous work. Throughout the book the writer included cutesy little side comments (usually in parentheses) which I'm sure she thought were humorous. I didn't find them funny; they seriously detracted from the information she was trying to convey.

Which brings up a whole other question: Do we all find the same things funny? The answer to that is a loud, "NO!" When you come right down to it, humor is very subjective and very personal, which is why there is room in the world for comedians as widely different as Don Rickles, Woody Allen, Steve Martin, and Jerry Seinfeld. Or Roseanne, Rita Rudner, Lily Tomlin, and Ellen Degeneres.

Connie Emerson says in *The 30-Minute Writer,* *"The more dismal the situation, the greater the editorial clamor for humorous articles and columns."*

Because it works: Think about a situation you are or were involved in. Maybe a family holiday get together or a high school reunion. Find the humor in the event. Write a short piece *reporting* the humor. Don't try to write funny. See the humor and report it. ✸

30

What the Heck Is a Personal Essay?

Y ears ago after a wonderful trip to Disney World, I wrote a piece called "Don't Take Your Kids to Disney World." When I finished it, I knew it wasn't a short story or a nonfiction article. But I didn't know what it was or what to do with it.

Several years later I attended a workshop on writing newspaper columns conducted by Fran Weaver at the annual International Women's Writing Guild Conference. My Disney World piece fit nicely into the category of one episode for a column. But what, I wondered, do I do with one episode when I don't have a column?

Several years later I attended another IWWG workshop, Writing the Personal Essay conducted by Susan Tiberghien. After the first session, I finally knew what I'd written—a personal essay. (Coincidentally, that same month *Writer's Digest* published the first article I'd ever seen on the personal essay: "The Personal Essay Revealed" by Herbert Hadad September 1991.) I knew this was a genre that I had a natural affinity to write. I then wrote several more personal essays which were published in a newspaper in Maine. Several years after that I entered my Disney World piece in the *Writer's Digest* Annual Writing Competition; it placed in the top one hundred personal essays.

Here are some basic guidelines for writing a personal essay:

A personal essay is short, between 500 and 1,200 words, with most running between 600 and 800 words.

It is usually written in the first person.

First, the writer chooses a short personal experience (an anecdote) on any subject. Often the experience is a common, everyday happening, but it is an event that has become so meaningful to the writer that it has become a metaphor for a larger issue. The writer then incorporates fiction writing techniques such as dialogue and sensory detail to dramatically relate the anecdote.

A personal essay contains another essential element: a reflective quality through which the writer shows the emotions he or she faced as a result of the incident—a reflection. The writer explains what lesson she learned or what new awareness she gained from the experience.

I questioned whether to use the word "explains" in the last sentence because I don't want you to think this is a long, drawn-out explanation. Again, it is a "show; don't tell" sentence or phrase at the most.

Here's an example of the personal essay structure:

I wrote an essay titled "The Truth About Santa Claus" in which I described exactly what happened the day my then six-year-old daughter discovered that the discount store Santa Claus was a woman and asked the dreaded question, "Is Santa real?" I faced the emotional conflict: do I tell the truth or perpetuate the myth? I then explained how I answered that question to resolve the conflict and hopefully not emotionally traumatize my daughter forever. I concluded with what I learned from the situation and what I will say when I have a granddaughter who asks, "Is Santa Claus real?"

In "Don't Take Your Kids to Disney World" I use a slightly exaggerated situation to illustrate the "joys" of grown-up kids and role reversal of parents and children, and I leave the reader to ponder: who are the real kids in life?

A personal essay doesn't discuss life-altering issues. But through an incident unique to the writer, each presents a universal life lesson every reader can relate to and benefit from, something they can take from the essay. Personal essays make richer the lives of both the readers and the writers. They include a strong emotional quality. Emotion comes from writing with passion whether to convey joy, longing, frustration, anger, or humor. Writing with passion leaves the reader *feeling*, as well as understanding, your message.

Personal essays are not opinion pieces. Personal essays are not simply anecdotes—the narration of an incident with no reflection or conclusion containing a lesson learned or new awareness gained.

Now that you know how to write a personal essay, where do you submit it? A good starting place is newspapers, especially if the theme of your essay is a holiday or annual event. Personal essays are often published on the op-ed page or in the lifestyle section. Many magazines have a one page "guest" column which is actually a personal essay. And here's one more opportunity—you can always submit it to *NEWN*.

Because it works: Try writing a personal essay. Start with something you know very well, such as: why were you named what you were named? Do you like your name? Were you named after someone special? What does your name mean to you? Do you know other people with your name? Would you rather be named something else? What? ❁

31

Dramatic Nonfiction: Showing the Truth

The only how-to book available on this writing style, by Theodore A. Rees Cheney, is titled *Writing Creative Nonfiction.* Truman Capote, using this method for *In Cold Blood,* called it the "nonfiction novel." Gay Talese used this form in *Thy Neighbors Wife,* as did Tom Wolfe in *The Right Stuff.* Some reporters and editors refer to it as "the New Journalism." It's standard form for true crime writers. Now, it's not my usual style to both paraphrase and disagree with Shakespeare, but Dramatic Nonfiction by any other name . . . is misleading.

Let me define **dramatic nonfiction** before I explain why it doesn't smell as sweet when called anything else. Dramatic nonfiction is the use of fiction techniques to tell a true story. It is *not* fictionalizing a true story (the form that starts with a kernel of truth and is embellished with fiction). It is *not* the technique of adding almost true (or supposedly true) descriptions, actions, and thoughts that aren't known to the author but are assumed to be true based on research of the subject.

Dramatic nonfiction is, or should be, objective journalism at its best telling only the truth that can be corroborated by written, verbal, or visual accounts of a person, place, or event. It's in the *telling* that dramatic nonfiction expresses a unique style. By using the same techniques that pique interest in a novel, we can show a true story with the flair of fiction.

Here's an example. While I was floundering around looking for the best style for my book *Private Lives of Ministers' Wives,* I stumbled upon *Thy Neighbors Wife* and was so impressed with both the true stories and the truth of those stories that I recognized the form I needed to tell Annie's story. I had what I thought was a good lead:

Annie Smith is 55 years old, the mother of six and had been married for 35 years to a United Methodist minister. Her waist-length, chestnut brown hair and the lively sparkle in her eyes belie the fact that four years ago, she attempted suicide. She tried twice to kill herself before anyone, including Annie, discovered they were treating the wrong person. It wasn't Annie who had to change. It was her husband Harvey.

Now, as leads go it isn't bad. It whets the appetite and promises a good story, but it just screams, "**Ordinary**!" After studying Talese, Wolfe, and Capote, I chucked that beginning and wrote this:

Annie chose a heavy plastic bag. It wouldn't do to have a thin, weak bag that she could easily tear with her fingernails. It had to be strong. She waited until Harvey was home. While he sat in the living room trying to release himself from the emotional tensions of his ministry, Annie went to the bedroom. She sat on the side of the bed and carefully unfolded the heavy-duty plastic bag.

. . . Annie pulled the bag over her head and shoulders. Harvey would be better off without her, she thought. He could spend all his time serving God if she weren't there to interfere. She wouldn't be around to distract him with her constant nagging and fighting for attention, commitment, support.

She wrapped the bag tightly around her, closing up any opening. Then she prayed for Harvey to find her before she died.

She could still breathe normally. There was enough air for her to analyze her ambivalent feelings. She wanted to die to help Harvey. Life would be easier for him with her dead. But, she didn't want to die. She wanted to live and be happy. She wanted her marriage to work. But the only way it could work, the only way Harvey could be happy, was for Annie to die.

There was still air in the bag. Annie took several deep breaths and felt a rising panic as the bag closed in on her face. Her heart pounded. She put her arms behind her and lay down on the bed pinning her hands under her back. Yes, dying was the only way.

The air in the bag was stale and warm, cloying. Getting air was difficult. Her breathing became quick and shallow, a reaction from both the lack of oxygen in the bag and her growing panic. The bag was almost tight against her face. She suppressed a desperate urge to rip it away. Her ambivalent feelings toward her own death rose again.

Where was Harvey? Didn't he notice stillness in the house? Wouldn't he question why she wasn't making dinner? Annie rolled slightly, side to side. First toward the pillows, then toward the foot of the bed. It was something to do so she wouldn't raise her arms and rip the bag from her face. Roll to the pillows. Roll to the foot. Back and forth, back and forth.

She was right. Harvey wasn't coming to help her. She'd be better off dead.

The plastic bag closed in on her face. All she had to do was open her mouth and take one long, last breath. The bag would close over her nostrils. The plastic forced down her throat would choke her. She steeled herself to do it. Harvey! Harvey! Where's Harvey?

Now that gets the reader's attention! With these two examples to compare, let's get back to our discussion on what's in a name.

To me, everything. Note how the second example, the one I used in the book, reads like a novel. It has suspense, background, conflict, characterization, setting, action, and plot. I used the "Where's Harvey?" theme in all the chapters about Annie. I started with a dramatic moment in Annie's life and then structured her story, and the balance of the book, around it showing the phases a ministerial marriage goes through while I showed the reader each step of Annie's journey. Like all good fiction, it's a story shown, not told.

Not one word is fictitious. Not one item, not one act, not one thought, not one detail did I create. The story is whole-cloth from Annie's experience as she told it to me in over one hundred hours of interviews. I didn't describe Annie because she wasn't thinking about how she looked while she lay asphyxiating on the bed. I didn't describe the bedroom because Annie never described it to me. Again, she wouldn't have noted the curtains, walls, or bedspread while she attempted to take her life. To include such details would be ludicrous and as contrived as the see-themselves-in-the-mirror scenes used in many novels to describe preening characters.

Although it reads like a novel, with all due deference to Mr. Capote, dramatic nonfiction is not "the nonfiction novel." There is no room in this form for anything fictionalized—not even the color of a dress.

I also object to Cheney's use of the term **creative nonfiction**. I do believe that all writing is creative. Creativity must be present in any writing to get a real or fictional story told in its best form. Ideal nonfiction is both entertaining and informative and creativity plays a big part in achieving that ideal. But the connotations of the word "creative" lead the reader to a belief that the form is more fiction than fact, more made-up than real. After all, creative writing courses don't cover nonfiction. Creative writing is the banner under which poetry, the short story, and the novel rest.

One of my crusades is to change the concept of creative writing to include all writing, thus giving credit to the nonfiction writers who also sweat blood finding just the right word and just the right way to tell their stories. But since this time has not yet come, I believe using the title "creative nonfiction" is misleading. It may nudge the writer to fictionalizing instead of using fiction techniques.

As for the term **new journalism**, this form is certainly not new. Capote, I believe, traced its use back to the eighteenth century when traveling British aristocracy sent back personal accounts of their journeys to the Continent. The form has been used ever since in features, magazine articles, and books.

There is a drawback to dramatic nonfiction: it's difficult! It's difficult to leave out all the description, action, dialogue, and inner thought processes so easily created for the novel but often unobtainable for Dramatic Nonfiction. Some writers offer a disclaimer with their books that certain nonessential elements have been made up—such as clothing. In the time elapsed since the event and the interview, the subject may have forgotten the exact outfit he or she was wearing. Yet the author describes an outfit and claims that what she described was selected only after determining the subject's normal style of dress and choice of color. I say if the subject can't remember what she was wearing on the day in question then it shouldn't be included at all. It's our job as writers to interview exactingly enough to obtain needed background and setting information to flesh out our real story with real detail—not fiction. These disclaimers make me suspicious about what else might have been fictionalized. Just as something ludicrous included in a novel makes me suspend my disbelief, these disclaimers make me suspend my belief in the veracity of the story told.

With this in mind, know that dramatic nonfiction requires excellent interview, note taking, and observation skills as well as knowledge of fiction technique and a nose for news. You need excellent research skills to find both primary sources (traveling to the scene, diaries, letters, conversations) and secondary sources (other books on the subject, magazines, and newspaper articles) to use this form. You need good interview skills to keep your subject on focus without appearing callous or hurried. You must be understanding but objective; empathetic but not sympathetic. All in all, expect research time to be double if not triple what it would be if you told your story in a more traditional journalistic style. And expect to be inundated by paper. Keep track of all your sources, notes, and details so that, if pressed, you can prove your claims. A paper trail is essential!

If it's so much work, why bother? Because the storyteller that exists in all of us is far more satisfied when we tell a story well than when we just tell it. The challenge is greater and when met well is supremely gratifying. My most satisfying moments are when I read Annie's suicide attempt to a group and hear them, caught up totally in the story, gasping for air as though they, too, had bags over their heads.

What's in a name? A big chunk of identity for starters. While I'll agree that a rose by any other name would smell as sweet, I still think the bloom of love would lose its appeal if we knew it as skunk cabbage. So forget the **nonfiction novel. Ignore creative nonfiction.** Steer away from the **new journalism.** It's **dramatic nonfiction** that smells—and reads—the sweetest.

Because it works: Ask a friend to describe her family's typical Thanksgiving celebration. Using your friend as the viewpoint character, *show* the reader how this family celebrates the holiday.

Here are some guidelines:

1.   You may record the interview so that it's easier to go back and determine exactly what your friend told you.
2.   You may go back and re-interview your friend for more details

Some don'ts:

1.   No one can think in this piece of writing. Not even your viewpoint character. You cannot "get into anyone's head" in this exercise.
2.   You **cannot** make anything up. You **cannot** add a juicy detail or two that came to you in a eureka moment. You **cannot** make up anything no matter how loudly the Muse yells. You can **only** write what you know from interviewing your friend.
3.   You **cannot** interview someone with whom you have spent Thanksgiving in the past. ❊

Article by Liz Aleshire

32

The Literary Story—I Don't Get It!

As writers we must also be readers. So out you go to buy a selection of magazines devoted to short stories. You buy *Ellery Queen, Alfred Hitchcock Mystery Magazine, Isaac Asimov, Mary Higgins Clark Magazine, Glimmer Train, The Antioch Re*view and, of course, *The New Yorker.*

You polish off the first four magazines quickly. You have no problem understanding what happens in the short mystery, sci-fi, and romance stories.

Then you pick up *The Antioch Review.* You read the first page of the first story. It doesn't grab you, so you try the second story. Same problem. You flip through the magazine reading opening paragraphs until you find one that at least holds your interest. You read and read until you realize you are just reading words. You have completely lost the train of the story—and there are another ten pages to go. "I thought these were supposed to be short stories," you cry!

You give up on the literary review and turn to *Glimmer Train.* You find one story about five pages long and force yourself to read the entire thing. "What was that all about?" you wonder when you get to the end. "I don't get!"

(You forget the stories in *The New Yorker* and just read the cartoons. Some of those you don't get either.)

What the heck is a literary story, anyhow?

To understand the literary story, you first have to understand the traditional plotted story. Whether presented as a written short story, a book, or a movie, the plotted story involves a main character who takes some action to resolve a conflict. It may be all action, all external conflict. In James Bond or Indiana Jones stories the plot is the thing (the adventure). The main character doesn't change; he resolves the external conflict. (And who would want James Bond or Indiana Jones ever to change?)

In other plotted stories there may be both external and internal conflict. By resolving the external conflict, the main character also resolves his internal conflict.

In Dickens's classic *A Christmas Carol*," Ebenezer Scrooge resolves the internal fears of the future shown to him by the Christmas ghosts by actions that show he is a changed man (bringing Christmas dinner to the Cratchits). At the end, all the loose ends are neatly tied up and the reader knows that Scrooge has truly changed.

In a literary story a character is wrestling with an internal conflict, which may or may not be resolved—quite probably it won't be. In *Beginnings, Middles, and Ends* (Writer's Digest Books 1993) Nancy Kress says that the "non-resolution is deliberate." She explains that the story examines a situation that may not be resolved because "the situation may be ambiguous and interesting in and of itself without resolution, or may be impossible to resolve."

"The whole point of contemporary literary short story," she continues, "is to present a question minus the answer."

Although you may think that nothing happens in a literary story, what should happen is that an emotional response will resonate within you. The story will evoke a strong feeling because it "sets off a complex intellectual and emotional reaction to the sensitive, skillful reader." It should "strike a cord of recognition and meaning in the reader." (Kress)

As you're reading a literary story, also notice the use of language. It will be more poetic, more descriptive. The writer will use vivid visual images and be more apt to include other sensory details in the description. And look for strong use of symbolism. A spider web isn't just a spider web. It's a symbol of the character inextricably caught in her life situation. The tree heavy with foliage outside the main character's window is more than a tree; it represents the Tree of Life, the Tree of Knowledge, the Family Tree, or some other philosophical tree.

The destruction of a spider web doesn't mean that the main character has decided to become Ms. Perfect Housekeeper. It more probably symbolizes how quickly life can be destroyed by a gust of wind. And the last leaf falling from the tree doesn't mean that it's time to do yard work. As the last leaf floats slowly to the ground, the main character breathes his last breath; and you, the Sensitive Reader, make the connection. (Yes, literary stories tend be on the downside.)

To teach this information to my fiction classes, I invite my writing buddy Jim Calandrillo to be my guest speaker. Jim is a literary writer. He illustrates (show; don't tell) the relationship between the plotted story and the literary story like this:

|_____|

Plotted story: Literary story
   Action and   Resolution and
   Symbolism   Resonance

   External conflict   Internal conflict

A story may fall anywhere on this continuum. It may include both internal and external conflict and various degrees of action, symbolism, resonance, and resolution. So if you're having trouble determining whether or not a story falls into the literary category, it may be because the story falls somewhere in the middle of the spectrum.

Jim uses Hemingway's "A Clean, Well-lighted Place" as a good example of a very short literary story—the kind of story which on first reading you may say, "But nothing happened." Read it again looking for internal conflict and symbolism. What emotion resonates through you after you read it?

Jim also uses the book *The Odd Sea* by Frederick Reiken as an example of a literary novel. Told from the point of view of a teenaged boy, the book deals with the internal conflict of his family after his older brother disappears. In a plotted novel, the main character would search, find clues, and discover what happened to his brother. That's not what happens in *The Odd Sea*.

Nancy Kress says that the literary story needs "a sensitive reader who makes subtle connections between the story and real life." You have to be willing and able to be a Sensitive Reader. So give it a try, keeping in mind that plotted means conflict and resolution while literary means symbolism and resonance. Put in the work by reading slowly and carefully. Look for the symbolism. Make the connections. Feel the emotion. So that when you're done, you can say, "It's a literary story—and I got it!"

Because it works: Pick a story from one of the literary publications mentioned above. Read it slowly and carefully, noting images, the conflict (or lack of conflict), the resolution (or lack of resolution). What questions does the story raise? Are they answered? How does the story make you *feel?*

Try writing a literary story. ❋

Article by Glenda Baker and Jim Calandrillo

33
Poetry 101

Here is Poetry 101—a crash course in the basics of poetry to help you determine what to look and listen for when you read a poem.

Rhythm and Meter: Most of us can recognize a poem because it looks different from prose. The lines may be very short and break where we don't expect them. Poetry also sounds different from prose because poetry has a definite rhythm. **Rhythm** is the natural beat that exists in words. When the number of beats is organized into a pattern, the result is called **meter**.

Classical poetic meters are comprised of two beats or three beats and are categorized by the arrangement of stressed (indicated by /) and unstressed (indicated by ~) beats. The two beat (or duple) meters are iambic, trochaic, spondaic, and dibrach.

An iambic foot is one unstressed beat followed by one stressed beat, as in:

~   /   ~   /
The Queen of Hearts,
~   /   ~   /
She made some tarts,

Trochaic is the opposite of iambic—one stressed beat followed by an unstressed beat
/   ~   / ~   / ~ /
Twinkle, twinkle, little star,
  /   ~ / ~   /   ~ /
How I wonder what you are.—Taylor

A spondaic foot is a foot with two stressed beats (//)
  /   /   /   /
Baa, Baa, black sheep,

/   ~   /~ /
Have you any wool?
 / ~ / ~
Yes sir, yes sir,
  /   / /
Three bags full.

A dibrach is a foot made-up of two unstressed syllables (~ ~) and not used frequently.

The main triple meters are dactyl, anapest, and amphibrach. A dactylic foot is made up of three syllables, a stressed followed by two unstressed:
/~ ~ /~ ~   /   ~ ~ /
Pussycat, Pussycat, where have you been?
/ ~   ~ / ~ ~ /~ ~ /
I've been to London to visit the Queen.

Anapestic is two unstressed syllables followed by a stressed syllable:

/~ ~   / ~ ~ / ~   ~   /
'Twas the night before Christmas, when all
  ~   ~   /
through the house
~ ~ / ~   ~ /~ ~ / ~ ~ /
Not a creature was stirring, not even a mouse;—Moore

Limericks are usually written in anapest.

Amphibrach produces a rocking rhythm produced by a stressed syllable between two unstressed syllables:
~ / ~   ~ / ~
To market, to market
~ / ~ / /
To buy a fat pig.

It's not important that you memorize these terms. What is important is to understand that different meters change the image created by the words. Here's an example from *The Poet and the Poem* by Judson Jerome:

      iamb: the HILL is GREEN and STEEP
      trochee: STEEP and GREEN is YON der HILL side
      spondee: STEEP GREEN YON HILL

anapest: over THERE is a HILL that is SHIM mer ing GREEN

dactyl: GREEN is the SHIM mer of HILLS at this AL ti tude

Meter can also refer to "a poetic foot". Combined with the number of feet per line such as mono (one), di (two), tri (three), tetra (four), and (penta) five, we then know that iambic pentameter means a line of five feet composed of one unstressed syllable followed by one stressed syllable.

Most importantly, the metrical form should enhance the imagery, the natural rhythm, and the content of the poem, not impose unnatural limits. Once the meter has been established (in the first line), it must remain the same throughout the poem.

Rhyme: the recurrence of similar sounds at the ends of words. We are most used to hearing rhyme at the end of lines. Internal rhyme, however, is the likeness of sounds at least one of which is not at the end of the line:

"But why can't I go?" Daniel wanted to know.

The rhyme scheme is the pattern of end rhymes as indicated by letters, such as: rhyming couplets: AABBCC cross rhyming: ABAB enclosed rhyming: ABBA terza rima: BAA BCB CDC

Rhyming should not limit or change the idea of the poem or the natural order of the words. One sure giveaway that a poet is inexperienced is forced rhyme that wrenches the words out of their natural order. For example, in the lines:

The old, bent man walked very slow

As along the highway he did go.

The words are inverted (*he did go*) from their natural order and sound awkward. These lines would sound more natural and still retain the meaning and image:

The man was old, his back was bent,

As down the dusty road he went.

Rhyme puzzles may be difficult, but solving them is part of the fun and challenge of writing poetry. Although a line or two may have to be completely rewritten, the poet often finds that the rewrite results in a more effective image.

The poet also considers other similarities in word sounds. **Alliteration** is the repetition of consonant sounds at the beginning of words: *Peter Piper picked a peck of pickled peppers.* Assonance is the repetition of vowel sounds: *Toy/noise/, oil/buoyant, mind/hide.* Consonance is the repetition of consonants other than at the beginning of words: *The towers and antennae on the routes and short cuts.* (The T sound is embedded in the words.) These repetitions of sounds that we look for in poetry would sound out of place in prose.

The language of poetry encompasses other kinds of recurrence: repetition of the same word or group of words, repetition of whole lines in various forms of such as the refrain in ballads, repetition of lines with a specific rhyme scheme within stanzas. (Stanzas are regular, consistent major divisions within a poem. Stanzas are loosely similar to paragraphs in prose.)

Poetry ranges from the very structured to the very free and open. Formal Japanese haiku, for instance, dictates not only the form but also the content. Each image must be expressed in only three lines of seventeen syllables—five in the first line, seven in the second, and five in the third. The content must deal with nature, such as this haiku by Ann Hendricks:

Red, blue, gold, black, grey.
Swooping from budding beeches,
Feathered rainbow feeds.

On the other end of the spectrum are **blank verse** and **free verse**. Blank verse does not rhyme, but is written in iambic pentameter. Shakespeare wrote predominantly in blank verse: *"What light from yonder window breaks?"* or *"To be, or not to be; that is the question:"*

Free verse also does not have end rhyme, a set structure, or a regular meter. But good free verse is not totally free; it may contain rhymes, natural rhythm or cadence, recurrence of other sounds and images. Good examples of free verse poems are "A Noiseless Patient Spider" by Walt Whitman and "The Love Song of J. Alfred Prufrock" by T. S. Eliot.

The subject matter of poetry is unlimited. A poem can be written about any subject or item—from "Paul Revere's Ride" by Longfellow to "To a Louse" by Robert Burns. What makes poetry unique is the use of similes and metaphors to create unique images. **Similes** are comparison using like or as (*The sun crossed the sky like a fiery chariot*), **metaphors** are comparison without use of like or as (*The sun is a fiery chariot crossing the sky.*)

The important thing is to pick one central metaphor to develop throughout the poem. Another example of an inexperienced poet is changing metaphors within a poem and/or mixing metaphors.

Poetry is intended to be enjoyed by being read out loud. So read it out loud. Enjoy the movement of rhythm and meter. Listen for the recurrence of sounds, words, lines. Be moved by the images created through metaphors and similes. Some poems are meant to tell a story; others are meant to present an image or are an exercise of sounds and plays on words.

Because it works: Find a familiar poem or nursery rhyme. Scan it to determine the rhyme scheme. Pick a rhyme scheme and write a poem using that scheme. ✾

34

ta DA, ta DA, ta DA, ta DA

What do William Shakespeare, Nikki Giovanni, Maya Angelou, Dr. Seuss and Shel Silverstein have in common? The obvious answer is that they are all poets. A less obvious answer is that these poets are favorites of mine. But dig deeper and I am sure you will discover there is something more that binds these and all good poets together.

Poetry is a genre that combines the variety of topic, the strength of format and the talent of personal style into the tightest, most succinct style of writing possible. Yet it's also the genre most novice writers think is easiest to write. But beware! There are certain clues that every poetry editor looks for to determine whether the hopeful poet is in a haste to get published or is truly a poet.

Let's follow the path of a fictional novice poet and learn which traps to avoid.

Step one: Our poet needs to find the right subject. There are five subjects that I call "safe subjects" because they are the first five subjects about which our poet would think to write:

1. **Love/Friendship Poems:** Almost every poet started off a poetry career by writing a special ode to his/her lover, spouse, parent, child, or best friend. When the person for whom the poem was written received the poem, s/he was overjoyed to be immortalized and lavished the writer with praise. Writing such pieces is truly a gift to give to the subject of the poem, but not necessarily for publication.

2. **Poems about writing:** With a sense of pride in the well-received friendship poem, our poet now sets off for a poetry career. However, staring at a blank pad of paper or computer screen without any new love about which to write causes the infamous "writer's block." Then, eureka! Why not write about how difficult writing is, or write about finding one's muse, or write about how others can avoid writer's block. Such poems can be worthwhile for the right market. *ByLine Magazine's* poetry section contains *only* poems about writing. But most poetry editors are looking for something deeper.

3. **Poems about gardens:** A full morning of writing "love poems" and "about writing poems" can leave our poet feeling a little stiff. Time for a nice walk outside through the neighborhood of well-cultivated gardens and lawns. Look at that beautiful rose bush (or iris plant or forsythia bush, etc.). It deserves to have a poem written about it. Yes, gardens are inspirational and there are several publications dedicated to home and garden decorating. Again, our poet needs to delve deeper.
4. **Sunrise/Sunset poems:** Depending on the time of day our poet prefers to write, the aforementioned walk through the neighborhood inevitably happens at dusk or dawn creating the inspirational water colored sky. However, like the garden poem, the sunrise/sunset poem doesn't find much commercial success.
5. **Depressing/Suicide poetry:** At this point, our poet decides to depart from the inspiring topics (since all four have been used up) and take a step into the darker side. Countless publications, probably too many, cater to a more sullen audience. Most poetry editors, however, are not looking for angst, complaints, or soapbox rantings.

Let's say that our poet is a step ahead of the rest. Our writer has found a unique topic—a week-old swig of milk in a gallon container in the fridge—this is where Step Two comes in:

Step Two: study the technical format of writing poetry. This is where our poet groans in disgust, remembering Mrs. Estes' ninth grade English class and all that confusing talk of metaphor, rhyme, meter, and free form. Wait a minute! The smile returns to our poet because there is a form called free form. Hold on! Before we get too excited, let's take a serious look at format:

1. **Free form:** Granted, e.e. cummings, William Carlos Williams, and Sylvia Plath had great careers writing free form verse. These poets seemed to simply transcribe what popped into their head and with no effort at all the masterpiece was complete. On the contrary, each successful free form poet struggles harder than any other writer to create tight works that capture a message without the help of a structured form. And the well-written free form verse probably goes through more revisions than any other type of poetry.
2. **Pick a format:** Our poet would do best to stay in the poetic playpen for a while by picking a classical format like a sonnet, a ballad, a haiku or, for a real challenge, a villanelle. Yes, these will take some hard work, so our poet would be wise to invest in a book like *Creating Poetry* by John Drury (Writer's Digest Books 1991). Working with a traditional form, inserting words like a jigsaw puzzle, will teach our would-be poet new words, better phrases, and more concise ways of saying things. This is exactly what poetry editors want to see.
3. **Find a Metaphor:** Finding a universal thought, idea, or philosophy for the unique idea in its classical format is our poet's next challenge. A poem about a clock is not just about a clock; it's about time running out or going too slow or not having

enough or having too much. As poet John Drury says, "Sight must lead to insight." Again, this extra step distinguishes a true poet from a writer who simply writes poetry.

So, what is the deeper meaning behind that old swig of milk in the fridge? Before answering, our poet will have watch out for a common trap . . .

4. **Avoid clichés!** A cliché is usually true (soft as a feather—yes, feathers are soft), but some clichés aren't proven (how do we know owls are wise)? Clichés are by definition trite or commonplace expression. Since it is already overused, our poet will want to avoid them at all costs and try an exercise like taking the phrase "soft as a _____" and filling the blank with twenty-five things that are soft. Then our poet should fill in the blank one more time and use that twenty-sixth idea. A poet digs deeper, past the obvious.

5. **Working with meter**: Luckily, most structured forms of poetry will dictate the necessary meter. Unfortunately, our poet's challenge is to keep the meter consistent throughout the poem. If our poet begins with a rhythm that goes:

ta DA, ta DA, ta DA ta DA

that's the way the entire poem has to continue. Our poet cannot change half-way through to:

DA ta, DA ta, DA ta Da

or to:

ta DA ta, ta DA ta

or any other meter. Our poet is locked in to the way the poem began. Yes, this is difficult and our poet will get frustrated. Hopefully, our poet will enjoy the challenge and not fall for another trap . . .

6. **Inverting the words** in a sentence to force a rhyme or rhythm. Here's an example of what our poet should **not** do:

Why do these questions pop into my mind?
Some day the answers I will find.

Do you think our poet speaks like that in real life? Of course not, so our poet will not want to write like that either.

So, what does our poet have? A unique subject, a central metaphor, a traditional format, and a consistent meter—everything that a poetry editor wants. And although for every rule in this article our poet could give me an example of how another poet broke that rule and wrote a great poem, I can give more examples of how following the rules will make our poet's writing stronger and marketable.

Now, friend and poet, comes the hardest part of all. Reread this article and replace the words "our poet" with the word "you." Then ask yourself, besides being poets and besides being some of Judy's favorites, what do William Shakespeare, Nikki Giovanni, Maya Angelou, Dr. Seuss, Shel Silverstein and I all have in common?

Because it works: Choose a well-known poem or song (children's nursery rhymes and Christmas carols work best) to rewrite. Keep the original format (the rhythm, stanza structure), but completely change the topic. When it's completed, ask a friend to read it aloud. Does it sound like the original song or poem? Can they guess the original piece? ✻

Article by Judy L. Adourian

35

Contests: Everybody Wins!

I've always liked entering writing contests because I never lose. I may not win, but I never lose. Contests give writers a chance to learn a number of things and any time you learn something, you win! Here are some of the things you'll learn by entering contests:

Learn to follow the rules. Does the contest want a blind copy with your name, etc. only on a cover sheet? When's the deadline? What's the entry fee? Making sure you follow all the rules is good practice. Nobody wants to be disqualified for printing on both sides of the paper when the contest requires one side only, or for entering more than one story when the rules say "just one."

Learn to write to a specific length. Let's say that the maximum word length for a particular contest is 1,000 words, but your story is 1,125 words? I bet you can cut 125 and not even miss them. I have helped students tighten stories they were sure couldn't possibly be cut by another syllable. (A few condensing hints: Use contractions when possible, use a semi-colon instead of a conjunction, change Apple Tree Lane to Applewood Lane.) It's amazing how much you can tighten your writing without changing your intent or meaning.

Learn to write for a deadline. Every contest has a deadline, which usually means entries must be postmarked by a certain date. Make sure you meet that deadline. As long as it is postmarked on the correct date, don't waste money sending your entry any way except first class.

Does sending your entry early in the contest period mean you're more apt to win? It shouldn't. At *NEWN* our judges don't read the entries until they are all in. But that doesn't mean you should wait until the last minute. Some contests increase the entry fee for last minute entries.

Learn to wait patiently. Contest winners are announced when they are promised, but you'll still have to wait until that time.

Worcester Magazine is a freebie available at a store that I don't go to very often; so when I saw a copy during the first week in June, I picked it up. I wondered if their annual short story contest was still being held, and sure enough, I saw a small announcement saying, "Don't forget the deadline for the short story contest is June 15th." I looked for the rules, but they weren't in that issue. I went on-line, but found no mention of the contest. I called the magazine and asked the gentleman in charge of the contest if I could enter more than one story. He said he didn't see why not, so I mailed in three. (There was no entry fee.)

Then I talked to a writer friend who had seen the rules and only one entry was allowed. Not wanting to be disqualified, I wrote a letter to the contest people explaining what had happened, asking them to withdraw my other entries, and to consider only the story I was now submitting (the one I thought was the best of the three.)

What did I have to lose? If I was disqualified, so be it. But I wasn't about to give up.

I then went away for a week and literally did forget about the contest.

Then on June 27th the phone rang. It was the gentleman from *Worcester Magazine* telling me my story had won second prize!

Being the editor-in-chief of *NEWN* doesn't exempt me from being ecstatic when my own writing wins a prize. I was surprised and extremely delighted.

So what's the lesson? The best thing about contests is that you never get a rejection slip, you always have the chance of winning, and *you'll* never lose!

Because it works: Find a contest, follow the rules, and enter it. You can't lose and you just might win! ❊

THE NEXT STEP—BECAUSE IT DOESN'T STOP WITH THE WRITING

36

The 30-Second Commercial for Fiction AND Nonfiction

I've been a part-time writer for three decades. I've sold over five hundred magazine and newspaper articles, four books, and I'm working on my fifth. I made those sales using the 30-second commercial. It's an efficient and effective way to increase sales and keep your mind focused.

The 30-second commercial is a sales pitch. It's short—less than two hundred words. You can use the 30-second commercial to pitch your book, short story, or article idea verbally, or use it as a query letter to a publisher or an agent. It's the beginning of the synopsis or overview of your novel or nonfiction book proposal. It is the very core of your story, book, or article containing only the theme, the primary characters, and the primary conflict or basic argument of your idea.

The best way to learn how to write a successful 30-second commercial is to read book jacket blurbs—those short paragraphs on the back of a paperback novel or on the front flyleaf of the dust jacket of a hardcover.

You'll need a special style of writing for your 30-second commercials. It's sales pitch language. It's different from what you usually write, but with a little practice, you can master it. Here are a few examples. In each one, I've boldfaced the sales pitch language.

This is from Zita Christian's romance novel *Just a Miracle*, published by Harper Monogram:

> *From the minute handsome medicine-show man Jake Darrow appeared in her small Montana town of Coventry, Brenna McAuley had no doubts he was a charlatan. Using scientific method and logic, the lovely young pharmacist set out to disprove his secrets of his outrageous claims. Still she never guessed that Jake's persistence would unveil hidden secrets of her own.*

Coventry was Jake's last chance to raise money for his ailing friend. First, he had to persuade the formidable Miss McAuley that he meant no harm. But he soon discovered that Brenna's spirited intelligence was not only thwarting his every maneuver, but igniting in him a surprising desire.

Note the use of active verbs, concrete nouns, and specific adjectives. Verbs like **disprove** are loaded with strong sales pitch language. **Unveil, thwarting, igniting** evoke stronger images than if the write: **prove him wrong, showed, blocked his path, or excited him.** The use of concrete nouns such as **charlatan, scientific method, logic, intelligence,** and **maneuver** also create strong images. Even the adjectives in this blurb are specific and tempting: **outrageous, hidden, spirited,** and **surprising**. The blurb also introduces the female and male protagonists and the main conflict of the novel. The real key is that it does it in only six sentences—only 104 words!

Here's one from *Night's Landing* by Carla Neggers published by Mira Books:

Archeologist Sarah Dunnemore is prepared for almost anything when she returns to her family home in Night's Landing, Tennessee, except the news that her twin brother, Rob, has just been seriously wounded in a sniper attack in Central Park. She rushes to New York to be with him, only to come up against no-nonsense Nate Winter, who was slightly wounded in the attack.

In his work as a deputy U.S. marshal, Nate is the best, but he's willing to break the rules to track down his and Rob's would-be killer. Nate believes the official investigation is going in the wrong direction—especially when he learns that Sarah is like a surrogate daughter and a confidante of her family's famous Night's Landing neighbor—the president of the United States.

When Nate suspects that Sarah has held back crucial information, he follows her to Night's Landing. Because Nate will let nothing—not his and Sarah's growing attraction for each other, not the mounting danger they face—stand in the way of the truth. But in a place filled with betrayal, greed and long-held secrets, truth is guarded with a deadly vengeance.

This blurb is slightly longer at 189 words and seven sentences, but still contains only the prime elements of the novel. The female protagonist is introduced in the first paragraph along with the precipitating event of the book: the sniper attack in Central Park. The second paragraph introduces the male protagonist and his conflict with Sarah. The last paragraph is loaded with strong pitch language: **betrayal, greed, long-held secrets, truth, deadly vengeance.**

Let's look at the blurb on a nonfiction book. This is from *Gifted Grownups: The mixed blessings of extraordinary potential* by Marylou Kelly Streznewski published by Wiley:

Gifted Grownups, Marylou Kelly Streznewski's unprecedented, 10-year study of 100 gifted adults, examines how being identified as a "smart kid" early on affects career choices, friendships and romantic pairings later in life. Why do some talented and gifted people become Mozarts and Einsteins or corporate chieftains, while others drop out of school, struggle to hold down jobs, or turn to self-destructive behavior? What are the signs of giftedness, its pitfalls, and its promise? Marylou Streznewski provides answers to these and other questions, and creates an intriguing picture of what it is like to have an accelerated mind in a slow-moving world.

This 30-second commercial immediately establishes the author as an expert: **Ten-year study, one hundred gifted adults**. Then, it states the book's thesis: **being gifted can affect everything in a person's life**. It then asks several questions designed as teasers to capture the reader's attention. It ends with the promise of answers. Once again, it is the use of active verbs, strong nouns, and specific adjectives that hook the reader.

In my book, *Private Lives of Ministers' Wives* with Rev. Sherry Taylor, published by New Horizon Press, the editor chose to use, almost word for word, my 30-second commercial as the book jacket blurb:

They are unsophisticated, plain, dowdy, selfless, unassuming and timid. They are perfect wives, perfect mothers, and perfect church members. They are ministers' wives.

But are they really that perfect?

Peeling away the stereotypes, Liz Aleshire and Sherry Taylor reveal the women of the parsonages as imperfect personalities with real problems and prejudices.

This 30-second commercial started by stating the stereotype: ministers' **wives are perfect**. Then comes the question to form the basis of the argument: **but are they really perfect?** Then the sales pitch language: **peeling, reveal, imperfect, personalities, real,** and **prejudices.**

The 30-second commercial isn't just for book length writing. You can use the same active verbs, concrete nouns, and specific adjectives to sell a short story or article as well. In fact, writing a 30-second commercial for any project you're working on will solidify the concept and keep you focused on what your book, story, or article is about. It won't completely eliminate an occasional writing tangent or two, but it will probably keep you more on track than if you didn't have it.

Mastering the 30-second commercial will put you light years ahead of your writing competitors. Imagine for a moment that you are an agent attending a conference where ten-minute pitch sessions are offered. You have ten appointments scheduled. One writer appears for the appointment and says, "Well, I have this idea, see, about this woman. She's smart and about thirty. She's either named Marsha or Lolita, I haven't decided on a name for her yet. And, I don't know yet what she does for a living but I'll figure that out later. So, she meets this really attractive man and she, like, well, you know, falls in love, but then they have all these obstacles to overcome, but they do and get married in the end. Isn't that a great?"

Don't laugh. I've talked to agents who've had writers come to appointments unprepared, nothing written down, the basic information still sketchy, even without a business card! Now imagine that the next person on your list comes with a 30-second commercial written on an index card and reads it to you. The protagonist has a name and an occupation. Nothing is left to figure out later. The 30-second commercial is succinct, exciting, teasing. You want to know more. The prepared author hands you the index card along with a business card that lists her/his address, phone number, and e-mail.

So, which author would you ask to send in a proposal? That's right—the author who came prepared. The prepared author exudes professionalism while the unprepared author ends up rejected.

Here's how to master the art of writing the 30-second commercial: First, take a trip to your local bookstore. If your novel is a mystery, concentrate on the mystery section of the bookstore. If you've written a how-to, stay in that section. Now, pull book after book—at least twenty-off the shelves and read the blurbs. Write down the verbs, nouns, and adjectives that impress you the most. Then, with all that blurb language in your mind, write a 30-second commercial for the project you're currently writing. Yes, it'll take some practice. No, it's not easy. But, I want you to remember: You *can* do this—and you should!

Because it works: Below is a very bad example of a 30-Second Commercial for a Contemporary Romance. Your assignment is not only to put it into sales pitch language and make it interesting, you must also make it conform to the *rules* of the contemporary Romance genre. Have fun!

Frumpy and dumpy mechanic Gertrude Funkwalter thinks she's found love when the bus she rides daily has a flat tire and the driver doesn't know how to fix it. While she changes the tire, driver Herbert Monk thinks about a life with Gertrude. Such talent she has for changing tires!

But Gertrude really wants to be a tire changer for NASCAR driver Dale Jarrett and can't decide if love with Herbert will make that impossible. She almost decides she doesn't want him and will start her career as a NASCAR tire changer instead. Herbert can't think of any way to get her to his side.

And so the adventure begins. Two mousy people with unclear goals have a bunch of unusual things happen that stop them from having a love affair! ❈

Article by Liz Aleshire

37

The Necessary Evil

Recently I submitted a humorous personal essay to my local newspaper for publication consideration. That night, as I drifted off to sleep, I realized that I had neglected to include a self-addressed stamped envelope with my submission. The irony that I had made the same mistake that as an editor for *NEWN* annoys me the most (a submission without a SASE) caused me to laugh. What else could I do? I had to take the situation with a grain of salt. I sent a follow-up mailing to the newspaper the next day. Submitting the completed manuscript—it's the necessary evil. And there are a great many lessons to be learned from this process of paper cuts and broken egos.

In his book *The Playwright's Survival Guide: Keeping the Drama in Your Writing and Out of Your Life* (Heinemann, Portsmouth, NH, 1999) Gary Garrison says:

Let me tell you how much I hate submitting my plays to a theatre for their consideration: I'd almost rather walk a mile on a broken leg before I did it. It takes everything I've got to get it together to shoot one small script out to some small theatre in the mail. And if I'm skillful in finding ways to avoid writing a play, I'm brilliant when it comes to creating avoidance for sending them out. So let's collectively get it out of our systems now:

YES! WE HATE IT!
NOBODY WANTS TO DO IT! (We'd rather be discovered)
IT TAKES TIME!
THE RESULTS CAN BE REALLY FRUSTRATING!
IT'S EXPENSIVE!
THEY PROBABLY WON'T READ THE DAMN PLAY ANYWAY!
WE HAVE TO BE ORGANIZED!
WE HAVE TO . . . (gulp) SELL OURSELVES AND OUR PLAY.

Even if you don't want to have your work published or to become a rich and famous author (I'm speaking to all two of you out there), mailing out your work to a family member or friend to read is essential. Because as Liz Aleshire advises her students, in that nanosecond between the contents still being your property and it being owned by the postal service, you will suddenly remember the comma you left off of page 12, or the misspelled word on page 62, or the character flaw in your protagonist that suddenly makes your whole premise null and void. But alas! By the time your brain catches up with your hand, the manuscript slips away into the irretrievable federal postal abyss.

It's okay. You've learned lesson #1: Mailing out your work is the greatest editing process. Go back to your computer and revise your manuscript with these postal revelations before you send it out again.

Lesson #2 kicks in after your manuscript has been mailed. You've heard the cliché before: "Patience is a virtue." And it is—for other people. But you are a writer and it's been a week since you mailed out your manuscript. You know for a fact that mail only takes two days to get from your state to theirs. Sure the guidelines said four to six weeks turnaround time, but that's for other writers, not fantastic writers like you. Resist the urge to call the publisher. Learn lesson #2: Forget about it. The best thing you can do for yourself is to move on to another writing project. "A watched pot never boils." Get cooking on another story, essay, poem, or play. "Don't put all your eggs in one basket." Invite the muse to fill another basket of creativity. Maybe this next story will be THE piece that lands you on Oprah. Turn your attention elsewhere and go for it.

Besides, sometimes the most amazing things happen when we just let go. Take the case of Mary. She sent something to a magazine called "Ideals." She never heard back. And when I say she didn't hear back, I'm talking three decades passed! Yes, that's right, thirty years later she saw her piece in the most recent issue of "Ideals." Apparently she had moved a couple times in those thirty years (go figure) and the publisher hadn't been able to get in contact with her. She contacted the magazine and got paid. Imagine if she had waited anxiously at the mailbox every day for those thirty years waiting for a response!

It's like a joke that a friend of mine from college and I share. The punch line is "And he still hasn't called." Any woman who has ever dated knows exactly of what I speak. You go on a date, you have a good time, he promises to call you, he never does. Good thing we didn't sit around waiting for those calls or neither of us would have met the men who became our respective husbands.

Last, but not least, comes Lesson #3: Rejection bites, but it doesn't kill. A year ago I sent a poem to a magazine, which for their benefit I will leave nameless. My rejection came on a 4" x 4" piece of pink paper with two words typed in black, 18 point, Times New Roman at the top: "Not Quite." The bottom displayed the magazine name and address. Not even a form letter on a full sized sheet of paper! Painful? Yes. Discouraging? Absolutely. The end of my writing career? Hardly.

Through my company Stage Fright Playwrights, I offer a One-Act in One Year Correspondence workshop. Each month my students receive a playwriting and a marketing assignment. By the end of one year, my students have a completed manuscript and a list of theatres to send it to. Here's what I advise when it's time to send the finished play out:

Keep a record of the manuscript's title, where you sent it, the day you put it in the mailbox, and the theatre's estimated turnaround time (if one was given—not taking it seriously if it was). Should you find that you do not receive a response in six months, feel free to follow-up with a short note inquiring about the status of your work. Include your name, the manuscript's title, when you mailed it, and your understanding that they are busy and cannot always respond quickly. Include a SASE postcard in your letter with the following three options for the publisher to check off:

1. Your manuscript was never received; please send us a new copy.
2. Your manuscript has not yet been read.
3. Your manuscript has been read, we would like to publish it.

If you don't hear anything again for another six months, find another place to send your work. Remember, in this day and age, many small time publishers come and go far too quickly. Also, don't take one publisher's rejection personally. If your manuscript is returned with a letter that says: "We are not interested," find another place and send it out again. Document each time you get a response. It will make your manuscript that much more sensational when the public learns fifty-two other publishers passed it up!

Meanwhile, if you get some constructive criticism from a publisher (like you get when submitting to *NEWN*), take it seriously like you would any other feedback source. Consider the editor's suggestions. If they make sense to you, use that feedback in a revision of your piece and resubmit the new and improved version. The greatest satisfaction I receive as an editor is to receive a revised piece from an author who took the time to seriously consider suggestions I have made on a previous draft. Helping such potential, conscientious, and dedicated writers get published is a win for the writer, the editor, and the reader.

But if the submission process still manages to get you overwhelmed or discouraged, go to the library. Look up any famous writer and read reviews of their works. Masters have had flops. Amateurs have had one hit wonders. You'll never know what you can accomplish if you give up after one manuscript return. Or even after thirty.

So research some markets, print out your manuscript, buy your stationery supplies and stuff those envelopes! If you get a paper cut, cover it with a clear Band-Aid and show your writer's group your battle scar with pride. Walk boldly to the post office. Get to know your post office staff on a first name basis. And know that whether the publisher accepts your piece or not, the lessons you are learning during this necessary evil process make you a better writer.

Because it works:

Part 1: Create your own Submission Tracker. Include the following information:
Genre (Personal Essay, Short Story, Poem, etc.)
Title
To (Name, Address, E-mail, & Website of publication)
Found (a note regarding where you found this market)
Sent By (E-mail or Postal Mail—if by postal mail, include amount postage paid)
Date Submitted
Expected Turnaround Time or Deadline Date/Winners Named for contest entry
Response (date manuscript was returned or accepted)
Notes (place to include any extra information)
    Each time you submit a piece of writing, fill out all the information listed above.

Part 2: Set a submission goal. Vow to submit one piece of writing a week for a month. Use this as an opportunity to practice submitting your work and to try out your Submission Tracker. Keep your Submission Tracker Sheets and the responses you receive (whether accepted or returned) from publishers in a marketing binder. When the month is up, go back to the beginning of Part 2. ❁

                                        Article by Judy L. Adourian

38

Agents: Do You Need One, How To Find One, & What To Do With One!

*T*o *the Editors of NEWN:*

I was wondering, could you help me unravel a mystery? (It's a mystery to me, anyway.)

How does one find an agent—specifically for a YA [young adult] novel series? I read one article in the 2000 Guide to Literary Agents *that said your best bet is by word of mouth. Considering my options are limited when it comes to word of mouth, where else would you suggest I turn?—M. O., Simsbury, Connecticut*

Do you really need an agent?

M. O.'s question is one that many writers have. All three *NEWN* editors agree that the answer is: Yes, no, and maybe.

Yes, because agents represent books, and most publishers will not consider a book unless it comes through an agent.

No, because agents do not handle short stories, magazine articles, poetry, or personal essays. Writers submitting to electronic publishers don't need an agent.

Maybe. Some writers have been published without the aid of an agent (such as in children's literature), but there are no guarantees.

How do you find an agent?

Word of mouth probably is the best way to find an agent. Ask every writer you know, published and pre-published. "I'm looking for an agent. Do you have one you'd be willing to refer me to?" Some published writers may not be willing to give out the name of their agent, but you'll never know unless you ask. Pre-published writers may know other writers who do have an agent. If you get a lead, be sure to ask the writer if you can use his/her name when you contact the agent.

Another suggestion is to go to a bookstore or library (bookstores are usually more current) and search for books similar to yours. Authors frequently mention their agents in their acknowledgements, which could turn into a lead. That agent may be willing to represent your similar book.

Agents frequently look for new talent at writing conferences, so be on the lookout at any conference you attend. Conferences are also a great place to network with other writers who may have an agent.

Search all *Guides to Literary Agents*. This is work, but you have to do it. Find the most recent copy, read what each is looking for, and make a list of those who represent your genre and fill your needs other ways.

Lastly, resort to the phone book. This is probably the least effective strategy because it will provide you only with a list of names, addresses, and phone numbers, but may not include more detailed information. The positive side, however, is that you may find a more local agent.

Now that you have a list of possibilities, you need to send simultaneous query letters to every agent on your list. The letter should be composed of three parts:

Part 1:   Tell the agent what you want.
Part 2:   Give a brief statement as to what your book is about and who your audience is.
Part 3:   Briefly mention your writing credits.

Be sure your query letter includes your name, address, phone number, and e-mail address.

A sample letter might read:

I am looking for representation for the first in a series of YA novels. Searching for Home *is 130,000 words and is completed. When 10-year-old Jimmy Brown loses both his parents in a car accident, he is sent to a series of foster homes. At each house, he encounters a specific conflict and learns how to deal with it. But Jimmy never feels welcome, accepted, or loved. When he finally meets Hester, a homeless bag lady, he experiences love and acceptance for the first time and learns lessons that will help him the rest of his life.*

Future volumes in this series will deal with . . . .

I have a chapter-by-chapter synopsis and the first three chapters available.

Credits: previously published books and articles. (I am the author of_____ and my work on foster care has appeared in ___.

If you don't have any published credits, don't say so. Just omit this part.

Other pertinent background information that gives you credibility on the subject:

I've been a Children's Advocate for 15 years and have been the foster mother of three.

Enclosed is a SASE for your reply. (Don't forget the SASE*!*)

Do not send any portion of your book with your query letter.

Now comes the hard part: Waiting for replies. Then decide which sounds best. This will be a subjective call based on the tone of the reply and how willing the agent is to see your work. What if more than one agent replies? (May you have this problem!) Take your time and think about each agent's reply. Don't think you have to respond immediately to the first one you hear from (although you'll want to!). Give it some time. You may hear from two or three more.

If the agent is interested in your work, he or she will tell you what to do next: how much of the book to send. Usually agents want to see the first three chapters and a synopsis of the rest of the book. Send what the agent asks for. (Don't send chapters 5, 17 and 32 because you like them better than the first three. Maybe this is the time to rewrite 1-3.)

A novel should be completed before you contact an agent. A nonfiction book should be a work-in-progress to the point where you have done enough research to know that you have sufficient material for a book and that you can immediately supply the agent with the first three chapters and an outline.

Why do you need an agent?

Many publishers will accept submissions only through an agent, so having one may be the only way to get your work to a publisher.

As a writer, you probably don't have the time or the desire to research the markets. An agent knows the markets and has contacts with many publishers. She will promote your work to the right publishers. If she finds an interested publisher, she will be the contact person. She will negotiate all financial dealings, and all rights issues.

An agent works on commission which is usually 15% of what the publisher offers the writer. This may sound like a lot, but it's worth it when you consider all the work you don't have to do.

Red flags!

Most agents do not charge a fee to read your manuscript. They earn their commission through the work they do to sell your book. Most agents also do not refer writers to an editorial service that will charge the writer for possibly unnecessary editing. The aim of being published is to get paid for your work. If an agent asks you for money in any form, look for a new agent.

Remember—an agent works for you. It is his/her job to find the best market for your work. A good agent is worth every dollar she earns.

Because it works: Imagine that your novel is finished. Talk to published writer friends about how they got their agent. Research *Guides to Literary Agents*. Find five agents that represent your genre. Go to a conference, listen to agents, and actually speak to one! ✳

Article by Glenda Baker and Liz Aleshire

39

A Different Breed of Editor

"*Oh, here's another submission from Jane Doe!*"
"*Oh no, not another submission from Jane Doe!*"

Periodically editors write columns about things that annoy them. Sometimes they write humorous lists of how to annoy an editor so you'll know what you are not supposed to do. Sometimes they write scathing articles with a tone of "these things annoy me and if you do them I will never, ever publish your work." Sometimes they mean it.

Anyone who reads writers' magazines can list the usual thorns in an editor's side: get the editor's name wrong, don't include a SASE, single-space your manuscript, etc., etc., etc. You've seen the lists, and I'm sure you try your best not to commit these grievous offenses.

We, your *NEWN* editors, consider ourselves a different breed of editor. We are first and foremost teachers. Liz and I both teach in continuing education programs. Liz, Judy, and I all teach at the annual International Women's Writing Guild Conference. We all feel that instructing novice writers in the proper way of doing things is part of our job. But we are also human and from time to time we get annoyed. We usually have a good laugh about it, but sometimes that just isn't enough. Recently we boiled all our pet peeves down to one basic peeve which can be summed up in one admonition: **be professional!**

No matter how new or old you are to the writing game, act professionally—even if you don't feel you are a professional. Or in other words, do the things professionals do and you will become professional.

Professionalism is not a matter of how long you've been writing or whether or not you've ever been published or are paid for your work. Professionalism is an attitude that says, "I know the rules apply to me, and I will abide by them."

Obviously, that means following all the rules of standard submission procedure, and it means following the guidelines of each publication you submit to. The word length and submission period applies to *you*. You are not an exception. If you think you are, you will annoy an editor.

Here are some things that have recently taken up my time, time I'd rather have spent on other things. I get annoyed when I have to do things that I feel I shouldn't have to do and can't do the things I want to do (like write weird stories.)

1. If an editor returns your submission for whatever reason, do not write to the editor to convince her that she should reconsider her decision. She has made her decision. End of discussion.

    Now, I did not waste time corresponding another time with the writer who sent me a "please reconsider" letter, but just reading her letter annoyed me and put me in a grouchy mood. It's not nice to put an editor in a grouchy mood.

2. When you submit your manuscript, we assume you are sending your best work possible. After you have submitted your work, you will inevitably think of a better word choice, a better phrase, a small bit of description you want to add. So, you think, a rewrite is in order and you submit another version

    Wrong! Do not send a rewrite. It screams insecurity and amateur. (Please understand that I am not chastising those of you who may have done this once. Just don't do it again.) A resubmission can also be confusing. "Didn't I just read this?" the harried editor wonders. Some days it takes very little to confuse a harried editor.

3. Especially after your work has been accepted and we have sent you a contract, you will again think of changes. But again, do not send a revision. And do not send three or five or seven revisions with letters explaining your changes. Your work has been accepted! Let it go! Start a new piece!

    We know that errors happen; and because we are writers too and submit our work, we are convinced that typos appear after manuscripts are mailed! We are not looking for perfection.

    We know perfection is impossible. We have proofreaders who read to find typos and factual errors. If we have a problem with a fact or a phrase, we'll check it, or we'll contact you.

4. Now that we're on the subject of perfection, I'll let you in on a secret: We are not perfect, either. Sometimes there's a typo in a letter we send to you or a manuscript gets lost or a subscription gets fouled up. We hate to make mistakes; but when we do, our goal is to handle them professionally.

    None of us will ever be perfect, but we all can and should try to be professional. The rules do apply to us all. Abide by them. When your manuscript arrives in the mail, we want to say, "Great! Here's another submission from Jane Doe!"

Because it works: Whenever and wherever you submit a manuscript, remember that you are a professional writer. *Be* professional! ✸

FINDING YOUR VOICE AND STYLE—
BECAUSE IT'S ABOUT YOU

40

Recognizing Your Style; Finding Your Voice

The first writers' conference I ever attended was in 1982. I was very new to writing; in fact, I didn't even consider myself a writer—just someone who liked to write. At many of the workshops I attended, the leaders mentioned "finding one's voice." I wondered what they meant.

In May of 1996 as I talked to the students in the final session of my short story course, I told them, "I've taught you all the mechanics of short story writing. Your assignment is to write, write, write, write. Now what you need is practice, practice, practice—and to find your voice as a writer."

As soon as I said it, I knew someone was going to ask, "And how do we do that?"

Sure enough, when I opened the class to questions and answers, Janice asked, "You said we have to find our voices as writers. What does that mean and how do we do it?"

I don't remember my exact off-the-top-of-my-head answer, but I know that during the discussion that followed, someone, probably Janice, asked, "Is voice the same as style?" adding another element to a subject that is hard enough to define.

Since then I've researched that question.

I first discovered that there are several kinds of voice for writers to deal with. The first that comes to mind is active voice and passive. And although I'm sure it's better to have an active rather than a passive voice, that's a matter of grammar, not the kind of voice I'm talking about.

Everything I read related voice to point of view, giving voice to characters. That's another use of voice but still not what I was looking for. So I had to give this one some deep thought. What I determined was:

Style has to do with how you write.

Voice has to do with who you are.

Your writing style involves how you use words and sentences, the flow and rhythm. Whether your sentences tend to be short and punchy or long and complex. Whether you tend to use long words or short words. Whether the natural tone of your writing is casual and conversational or more reserved and formal. Your style might change somewhat depending what kind of writing you are doing.

You may be unaware what kind of style you have—or if you even have one. It took me years to determine I had one. My natural style of writing is just what I'm doing now, chatting with you as if we were having a cup of tea in my kitchen. There are times when I have to concentrate on using a more formal style.

One way to start determining your style is to read ten things that you've written without stopping. If you get to number eight and you think, "All this stuff sounds the same," you may have found a clue to your style. Once you've identified that you do have a style, you can decide if you like it or if you deliberately want to change it.

Your voice as a writer is a whole different thing. Voice has to do with who you are, what you've experienced in your life, and how those experiences have affected you—all the things that make you the person you are—which make you the writer you are. These attitudes and beliefs, conscious and subconscious, run through all of your writing like an unseen undercurrent pulling you to an inevitable result.

Your writer voice answers questions like:

Do you view the world as a safe place or a scary place? Fascinating or unknowable? Challenging or defeating? Is the world full of wonderful, crazy weird things? Is life an exciting adventure? Or is life a bitch and then you die? Is it full of potholes, pit traps, and danger? Are the people you meet fascinating individuals through whom you can see a different side of life? Or are they all out to get you? Are people basically good or basically evil?

Is the cup half-empty or half-full? Is there water in the cup or wine or milk or Kool-Aid or champagne or hemlock? Is it a cup at all? Or is it a glass, a mug, a paper cup, a chalice, or a bucket? Is the bucket full to overflowing or is there a hole in the bucket, dear writer, dear writer?

Finding your voice is not just a matter of determining whether you're an optimist or a pessimist. We all are both depending on the day of the month, the time of the year, how close we came to winning last night's Megabucks, and what the reply was in the SASE that came back in today's mail.

Are you willing to take a risk in your writing? In the characters you develop? In the stories you decide to tell? In the topics you are willing to tackle?

One factor that will help you find your voice is to develop confidence in your writing. (Once again, this is why writers need other writers and small writing groups.) When you know you can handle the mechanical aspects of writing, you'll be willing to take more risk with the content. When you take that risk, your voice that had been whispering softly in the background will start to speak more loudly—eventually it will shout.

Because it works: Read ten pieces you wrote but haven't read in a while. Do they all feel the same in some way: same rhythm, same sentence structure, same word choices? Are they all chatty and casual or formal and reserved? This is your style. Do you like it? What do you want to change? Do you hear your voice coming through? Is it strong and confident? Is it tentative and shy? The more you write the stronger you and your voice will become. ❀

41

A Writer's Style; A Writer's Voice

Your style is **how** you write
  How you handle the mechanics of
    grammar, spelling, punctuation, and
      usage
  It's vocabulary and language
  It's sentence structure and syntax
    euphony and rhythm
    simile and metaphor
    onomatopoeia and alliteration

Style is Monet compared to VanGogh
  Mozart compared to Vivaldi
  Pavarotti compared to Sinatra
  Hemingway compared to Faulkner
  William H. Buckley compared to Dave
    Barry

You do have a style
  You may not be aware of it
  You may not recognize it yet
but you do have a style
  a style waiting to be developed

Your style should feel comfortable
  it's the natural way you write
Gradually you will become more aware
  of it.

DON'T FIGHT IT!
And don't let ANYBODY—writing group
    member, teacher, editor, critic,
    relative,
  tell you to change your style

Your style is a GIFT
Only you can
  develop it
  hone it
  perfect it
  use it to your advantage
Your style is unique. It is yours alone. It
  is you.

A writer's voice is not any one "character's
    voice"
  It is not "person" or "point of view"
  It's not the grammatical active or
    passive voice
  It is not "dialogue"
  Your writer's voice is **what** you write
  It is who you are,
  It is your personality but a whole lot
    more
  It's what you believe
  It's what you value

It's your philosophy of life and human
nature
It's what you know to be true and
what you know to be false
It's what you stand for and
what you will not stand for
It is what you have experienced in your
life
It is where you are and how you got
there
It is how you see the world

Your writer's voice is
what you give yourself permission
to write about, to read, to think, to
discuss
It's what you feel comfortable writing
about
It's what you feel uncomfortable writing
about
It's the risks you're willing to take
how far you're willing to go
Where you have to stop

Your writer's voice permeates everything
you write
even when you don't know it
even when you don't want it to
even when you deliberately try to hide it

Your writer's voice speaks through
everything you write
every character you create
every setting you choose
every word of dialogue you compose
each point of view you pick
how you begin
what happens in the middle
and how the story ends

You cannot change your voice and
You shouldn't even try

it is what you have to say
and your need to say it

But your writer's voice will change
as you grow and change
as you are willing to take more risks
in your life and in your writing
as you become more confident as a
person
and as a writer
Your voice will become louder
it will become stronger
And gradually you will hear it, too. ❄